Preface

Microsoft Azure Administrator AZ 104: Microsoft Azure Administrator is a meticulously structured guide designed to equip aspiring and experienced cloud professionals with the knowledge and practical skills required to efficiently manage cloud services within the Microsoft Azure ecosystem. As cloud computing continues to redefine modern IT infrastructure, the role of Azure administrators has become increasingly vital in ensuring seamless operations across storage, security, networking, and compute capabilities. This book serves as a comprehensive resource, aligned with the objectives of the AZ-104 certification exam, to provide an in-depth understanding of Azure administration tasks, including implementation, management, and monitoring of cloud environments. Through a methodical approach, this guide builds foundational knowledge and progresses toward advanced topics, ensuring that readers develop both theoretical understanding and hands-on expertise.

Beyond exam preparation, Microsoft Certification AZ-104: Microsoft Azure Administrator emphasizes real-world applicability, integrating practical exercises, case studies, and self-assessment tools to reinforce learning. Each chapter is structured to facilitate incremental learning, with review questions and key insights that enhance retention and application of core concepts. Additionally, supplementary resources such as online test papers and expert-led video tutorials further enrich the learning experience. Whether you are embarking on a career in cloud administration or seeking to refine your Azure expertise, this book provides the essential tools to confidently navigate the evolving landscape of cloud computing. We invite you to engage with this material, deepen your understanding, and take a significant step toward mastering Azure administration and achieving certification success.

Table of Contents

Chapter 1: Practice Questions &Answers Part 1

QUESTION 1
You need to recommend a solution to automate the configuration for the finance department users. The solution must meet the technical requirements. What should you include in the recommended?
A. Azure AP B2C
B. Azure AD Identity Protection
C. an Azure logic app and the Microsoft Identity Management (MIM) client
D. dynamic groups and conditional access policies
Answer: D

QUESTION 2
You discover that VM3 does NOT meet the technical requirements. You need to verify whether the issue relates to the NSGs. What should you use?
A. Diagram in VNet1
B. the security recommendations in Azure Advisor
C. Diagnostic settings in Azure Monitor
D. Diagnose and solve problems in Traffic Manager Profiles
E. IP flow verify in Azure Network Watcher
Answer: E

QUESTION 3
You need to resolve the licensing issue before you attempt to assign the license again. What should you do?
A. From the Groups blade, invite the user accounts to a new group.
B. From the Profile blade, modify the usage location.
C. From the Directory role blade, modify the directory role.
Answer: A

QUESTION 4
Which blade should you instruct the finance department auditors to use?
A. invoices
B. partner information
C. cost analysis
D. External services
Answer: A

QUESTION 6
You plan to deploy five virtual machines to a virtual network subnet.
Each virtual machine will have a public IP address and a private IP address. Each virtual machine requires the same inbound and outbound security rules. What is the minimum number of network interfaces and network security groups that you require? To answer, select the appropriate options in the answer area. NOTE: Each correct selection is worth one point.

Minimum number of network interfaces:

5
10
15
20

Minimum number of network security groups:

1
2
5
10

A. Mastered
B. Not Mastered
Answer: A

QUESTION 7
-(4)
This question is part of a series of questions that present the same scenario. Each question in the series contains a unique solution that might meet the stated goals. Some question sets might have more than one correct solution, while others might not have a correct solution.
After you answer a question in this section, you will NOT be able to return to it. As a result, these questions will not appear in the review screen. You have an Azure subscription named Subscription1 that contains the resources shown in the following table.

Name	Type	Location	Resource group
RG1	Resource group	East US	Not applicable
RG2	Resource group	West Europe	Not applicable
RG3	Resource group	North Europe	Not applicable
VNET1	Virtual network	Central US	RG1
VM	Virtual network	West US	RG2

VM1 connects to a virtual network named VNET2 by using a network interface named NIC1.
You need to create a new network interface named NIC2 for VM1.
Solution: You create NIC2 in RG1 and Central US. Does this meet the goal?
A. Yes
B. No
Answer: B

QUESTION 8
Note: This question is part of a series of questions that present the same scenario. Each question in the series contains a unique solution that might meet the stated goals. Some question sets might have more than one correct solution, while others might not have a correct solution.
After you answer a question in this section, you will NOT be able to return to it. As a result, these questions will not appear in the review screen.
You have a computer named Computer1 that has a point to site VPN connection to an Azure virtual network named VNet1. The point to site connection uses a self signed certificate.
From Azure, you download and install the VPN client configuration package on a computer named Computer2.

You need to ensure that you can establish a point to site VPN connection to VNet1 from Computer2. Solution: On Computer2, you set the Startup type for the IPSec Policy Agent service to Automatic.
Does this meet the goal?
A. Yes
B. No
Answer: B

QUESTION 9
Note: This question is part of a series of questions that present the same scenario. Each question in the series contains a unique solution that might meet the stated goals. Some question sets might have more than one correct solution, while others might not have a correct solution. After you answer a question in this section, you will NOT be able to return to it. As a result, these questions will not appear in the review screen. You have an Azure subscription named Subscription1 that contains the resources shown in the following table.

Name	Type	Location	Resource group
RG1	Resource group	East US	Not applicable
RG2	Resource group	West Europe	Not applicable
RG3	Resource group	North Europe	Not applicable
VNET1	Virtual network	Central US	RG1
VM	Virtual network	West US	RG2

VM1 connects to a virtual network named VNET2 by using a network interface named NIC1. You need to create a new network interface named NIC2 for VM1. Solution: You create NIC2 in RG2 and West US. Does this meet the goal?
A. Yes
B. NO
Answer: A

QUESTION 10
You have an azure subscription that contain a virtual named VNet1. VNet1. contains four subnets named Gatesway, perimeter, NVA, and production. The NVA contain two network virtual appliance (NVAs) that will network traffic inspection between the perimeter subnet and the production subnet.
You need to implement an Azure load balancer for the NVAs. The solution must meet the following requirements: The
NVAs must run in an active active configuration that uses automatic failover.
The NVA must load balance traffic to two services on the Production subnet. The services have different IP addresses
Which three actions should you perform? Each correct answer presents parts of the solution.
NOTE: Each correct selection is worth one point.
A. Add two load balancing rules that have HA Ports enabled and Floating IP disabled.
B. Deploy a standard load balancer.
C. Add a frontend IP configuration, two backend pools, and a health prob.
D. Add a frontend IP configuration, a backend pool, and a health probe.
E. Add two load balancing rules that have HA Ports and Floating IP enabled.

F. Deploy a basic load balancer.
Answer: BCE

QUESTION 10
-(4)
You have an Azure subscription that contains the resources shown in the following table.

Name	Type	Location
VNET1	Virtual network	East US
IP1	Public IP address	West Europe
RT1	Route table	North Europe

You need to create a network interface named NIC1. In which location can you create NIC1?
A. East US and North Europe only.
B. East US and West Europe only.
C. East US, West Europe, and North Europe.
D. East US only.
Answer: D

QUESTION 11
You have an Azure subscription that contains a user account named User1.
You need to ensure that User1 can assign a policy to the tenant root management group. What should you do?
A. Assign the Owner role to User1, and then instruct User1 to configure access management for Azure resources.
B. Assign the Global administrator role to User1, and then instruct User1 to configure access management for Azure resources.
C. Assign the Global administrator role to User1, and then modify the default conditional access policies.
D. Assign the Owner role to User1, and then modify the default conditional access policies.
Answer: A

QUESTION 12
You have an Azure subscription that contains the storage accounts shown in the following table.
You need to identify which storage account can be converted to zone redundant storage (ZRS) replication by requesting a live migration from Azure support. What should you identify?
A. Storage1
B. Storage 2
C. Storage 3
D. Storage 4

Name	Kind	Performance	Replication	Access tier
Storage1	Storage(general purpose v1)	Perminum	Geo redundant storage(GRS)	None
Storage2	StorageV2(general purpose v2)	Standard	Locally redundant storage (LRS)	Cool
Storage3	StorageV2(general purpose v2)	Premium	Read access geo redundant storage (RA GRS)	Hot
Storage4	BlobStorage	Standard	Locally redundant storage (LRS)	Hot

Answer: B

QUESTION 13
You have an Azure virtual machine named VM1. Azure collects events from VM1.
You are creating an alert rule in Azure Monitor to notify an administrator when an error is logged in the System event log of VM1. You need to specify which resource type to monitor.
What should you specify?
A. metric alert
B. Azure Log Analytics workspace
C. virtual machine
D. virtual machine extension
Answer: D

QUESTION 14
You have an Azure subscription that includes data in following locations:

Name	Type
Container1	Blob container
Share1	Azure files share
DB1	SQL database
Table1	Azure table

You plan to export data by using Azure import/export job named Export1. You need to identify the data that can be exported by using Export1. Which data should you identify?
A. DB1
B. Table1
C. container1
D. Share1
Answer: D

QUESTION 15
-(4)
You have an Azure Active Directory (Azure AD) tenant named contosocloud.onmicrosoft.com. Your company has a public DNS zone for contoso.com.
You add contoso.com as a custom domain name to Azure AD. You need to ensure that Azure can verify the domain name. Which type of DNS record should you create?
A. PTR
B. MX
C. NSEC3
D. RRSIG
Answer: B

QUESTION 16
-(4)
You have a Microsoft 365 tenant and an Azure Active Directory (Azure AD) tenant named contoso.com. You plan to grant three users named User1, User2, and User3 access to a temporary Microsoft SharePoint

document library named Library1.
You need to create groups for the users. The solution must ensure that the groups are deleted automatically after 180 days.
Which two groups should you create? Each correct answer presents a complete solution. NOTE: Each correct selection is worth one point.
A. a Security group that uses the Assigned membership type
B. an Office 365 group that uses the Assigned membership type
C. an Office 365 group that uses the Dynamic User membership type
D. a Security group that uses the Dynamic User membership type
E. a Security group that uses the Dynamic Device membership type
Answer: BC

QUESTION 17
-(4)
You have two Azure virtual machines named VM1 and VM2. You have two Recovery Services vaults named RSV1 and RSV2. VM2 is protected by RSV1.
You need to use RSV2 to protect VM2. What should you do first?
A. From the RSV1 blade, click Backup items and stop the VM2 backup.
B. From the RSV1 blade, click Backup Jobs and export the VM2 backup.
C. From the RSV1 blade, click Backu
D. From the Backup blade, select the backup for the virtual machine, and then click Backup.
E. From the VM2 blade, click Disaster recovery, click Replication settings, and then select RSV2 as the Recovery Services vault.
Answer: D

QUESTION 18
- (4)
Note: This question is part of a series of questions that present the same scenario. Each question in the series contains a unique solution that might meet the stated goals. Some question sets might have more than one correct solution, while others might not have a correct solution.
After you answer a question in this section, you will NOT be able to return to it. As a result, these questions will not appear in the review screen.
You have an Azure subscription that contains the following resources: A virtual network that has a subnet named Subnet1
Two network security groups (NSGs) named NSG VM1 and NSG Subnet1
A virtual machine named VM1 that has the required Windows Server configurations to allow Remote Desktop connections NSG Subnet1 has the default inbound security rules only.
NSG VM1 has the default inbound security rules and the following custom inbound security rule: Priority: 100
Source: Any
Source port range: * Destination: *
Destination port range: 3389 Protocol: UDP
Action: Allow
VM1 connects to Subnet1. NSG1 VM1 is associated to the network interface of VM1. NSG Subnet1 is associated to Subnet1. You need to be able to establish Remote Desktop connections from the internet to VM1.

Solution: You modify the custom rule for NSG VM1 to use the internet as a source and TCP as a protocol. Does this meet the goal?
A. Yes
B. No
Answer: A

QUESTION 19
-
You have an Azure subscription named Subscription1.
You have 5 TB of data that you need to transfer to Subscription1. You plan to use an Azure Import/Export job. What can you use as the destination of the imported data?
A. an Azure Cosmos DB database
B. Azure File Storage
C. the Azure File Sync Storage Sync Service
D. Azure Data Factory
Answer: B

QUESTION 20
-(4)
You have an Azure virtual machine named VM1.
You use Azure Backup to create a backup of VM1 named Backup1. After creating Backup1, you perform the following changes to VM1: Modify the size of VM1.
Copy a file named Budget.xls to a folder named Data. Reset the password for the built in administrator account.
Add a data disk to VM1.
An administrator uses the Replace existing option to restore VM1 from Backup1. You need to ensure that all the changes to VM1 are restored. Which change should you perform again?
A. Modify the size of VM1.
B. Add a data disk.
C. Reset the password for the built in administrator account.
D. Copy Budget.xls to Data.
Answer: D

QUESTION 21
- (4)
You have an Azure subscription that contains a user account named User1.
You need to ensure that User1 can assign a policy to the tenant root management group. What should you do?

A. Assign the Owner role to User1, and then instruct User1 to configure access management for Azure resources.
B. Assign the Global administrator role to User1, and then instruct User1 to configure access management for Azure resources.
C. Assign the Global administrator role to User1, and then modify the default conditional access policies.

D. Assign the Owner role to User1, and then modify the default conditional access policies.
Answer: A

QUESTION 22
-(4)
You have an Azure subscription that contains the resources shown in the following table.

Name	Type	Resource group	Location
Valut1	Recovery services vault	RG1	East US
VM1	Virtual machine	RG1	East US
VM2	Virtual machine	RG!	West US

All virtual machines run Windows Server 2016.
You plan to restore the backup to a different virtual machine. You need to restore the backup to VM2. What should you do first?
A. From VM2, install the Microsoft Azure Recovery Services Agent
B. From VM1, install the Windows Server Backup feature
C. From VM2, install the Windows Server Backup feature
D. From VM1, install the Microsoft Azure Recovery Services Agent

Answer: A

QUESTION 23
-(4)
You have an Azure Linux virtual machine that is protected by Azure Backup. One week ago, two files were deleted from the virtual machine. You need to restore the deleted files to an on premises computer as quickly as possible.
Which four actions should you perform in sequence?

A. Mastered
B. Not Mastered
Answer: A

QUESTION 24
-(4)
You download an Azure Resource Manager template based on an existing virtual machine. The template will be used to deploy 100 virtual machines. You need to modify the template to reference an administrative password. You must prevent the password from being stored in plain text.
What should you create to store the password?
A. Azure Active Directory (AD) Identity Protection and an Azure policy
B. a Recovery Services vault and a backup policy
C. an Azure Key Vault and an access policy
D. an Azure Storage account and an access policy
Answer: C

QUESTION 25
-(4)
You create an App Service plan named App1 and an Azure web app named webapp1. You discover that the option to create a staging slot is unavailable. You need to create a staging slot for App1.
What should you do first?

A. From webapp1, modify the Application settings.
B. From webapp1, add a custom domain.
C. From App1, scale up the App Service plan.
D. From App1, scale out the App Service plan
Answer: C

QUESTION 26
-(4)
You have an Azure subscription that contains an Azure Storage account named storage1 and the users shown in the following table.

Name	Member of
User1	Group1
User2	Group2
User3	Group1

You plan to monitor storage1 and to configure email notifications for the signals shown in the following table.

Name	Type	Users to notify
Ingress	Metric	User 1 and User3 only
Egress	Metric	User1 only
Delete storage account	Activity log	User 1 , User2 , and User3
Restore blob ranges	Activity log	User1 and User3 only

You need to identify the minimum number of alert rules and action groups required for the planned monitoring.
How many alert rules and action groups should you identify?

A. Mastered
B. Not Mastered

Answer: A

QUESTION 27
You have an Azure Migrate project that has the following assessment properties: Target location: East US
Storage redundancy: Locally redundant Comfort factor: 2.0
Performance history: 1 month Percentile utilization: 95th Pricing tier: Standard
Offer: Pay as you go
You discover the following two virtual machines:
A virtual machine named VM1 that runs Windows Server 2016 and has 10 CPU cores at 20 percent utilization A virtual machine named VM2 that runs Windows Server 2012 and has four CPU cores at 50 percent utilization
How many CPU cores will Azure Migrate recommend for each virtual machine?
Answer: A

QUESTION 28
-(4)
You need to create an Azure Storage account that meets the following requirements:
• Minimizes costs
• Supports hot, cool, and archive blob tiers
• Provides fault tolerance if a disaster affects the Azure region where the account resides
How should you complete the command?
A. Mastered
B. Not Mastered
Answer: A

QUESTION 29
-(4)
You have an Azure Active Directory (Azure AD) tenant named contoso.onmicrosoft.com. The User administrator role is assigned to a user named Admin1. An external partner has a Microsoft account that uses the user1@outlook.com sign in.
Admin1 attempts to invite the external partner to sign in to the Azure AD tenant and receives the following error message: "Unable to invite user user1@outlook.com – Generic authorization exception."
You need to ensure that Admin1 can invite the external partner to sign in to the Azure AD tenant. What should you do?

A. From the Roles and administrators blade, assign the Security administrator role to Admin1.
B. From the Organizational relationships blade, add an identity provider.
C. From the Custom domain names blade, add a custom domain.
D. From the Users blade, modify the External collaboration settings.
Answer: D

QUESTION 30
-(4)
Note: This question is part of a series of questions that present the same scenario. Each question in the series contains a unique solution that might meet the stated goals. Some question sets might have more than one correct solution, while others might not have a correct solution. After you answer a question in this section, you will NOT be able to return to it. As a result, these questions will not appear in the review screen. You have an Azure subscription that contains the following resources:
A virtual network that has a subnet named Subnet1
Two network security groups (NSGs) named NSG VM1 and NSG Subnet1
A virtual machine named VM1 that has the required Windows Server configurations to allow Remote Desktop connections NSG Subnet1 has the default inbound security rules only.
NSG VM1 has the default inbound security rules and the following custom inbound security rule: Priority: 100
Source: Any
Source port range: * Destination: *
Destination port range: 3389 Protocol: UDP
Action: Allow
VM1 connects to Subnet1. NSG1 VM1 is associated to the network interface of VM1. NSG Subnet1 is associated to Subnet1. You need to be able to establish Remote Desktop connections from the internet to VM1.
Solution: You add an inbound security rule to NSG Subnet1 and NSG VM1 that allows connections from the internet source to the VirtualNetwork destination for port range 3389 and uses the TCP protocol.
Does this meet the goal?
A. Yes
B. No
Answer: A

QUESTION 31
-(4)
Note: This question is part of a series of questions that present the same scenario. Each question in the series contains a unique solution that might meet the stated goals. Some question sets might have more than one correct solution, while others might not have a correct solution. After you answer a question in this section, you will NOT be able to return to it. As a result, these questions will not appear in the review screen.
You have an Azure Active Directory (Azure AD) tenant named Adatum and an Azure Subscription named Subscription1. Adatum contains a group named Developers. Subscription1 contains a resource group named Dev.
You need to provide the Developers group with the ability to create Azure logic apps in the Dev resource group. Solution: On Subscription1, you assign the DevTest Labs User role to the Developers group. Does this meet the goal?
A. Yes
B. No
Answer: B

QUESTION 32
-(4)
You have an Azure subscription that contains two virtual networks named VNet1 and VNet2. Virtual machines connect to the virtual networks. The virtual networks n on premises server named Server1 th configured as shown in the following table.

Virtual network	Address space	Subnet	Peering
VNet1	10.1.0.0/16	10.1.0.0/24 10.1.1.0/26	VNet2
VNet2	10.2.0.0/16	10.2.0.0/24	VNet1

You need to add the address space of 10.33.0.0/16 to VNet1. The solution must ensure that the hosts on VNet1 and VNet2 can communicate.
A. Mastered
B. Not Mastered
Answer: A

QUESTION 33
-(4)
You have an Azure subscription that contains the virtual machines shown in the following table.

Name	Operating system	Connects to
VM1	Windows Server 2019	Subnet1
VM2	Windows server 2019	Subnet 2

VM1 and VM2 use public IP addresses. From Windows Server 2019 on VM1 and VM2, you allow inbound Remote Desktop connections. Subnet1 and Subnet2 are in a virtual network named VNET1.
The subscription contains two network security groups (NSGs) named NSG1 and NSG2. NSG1 uses only the default rules. NSG2 uses the default and the following custom incoming rule: Priority: 100 Name: Rule1 Port: 3389 Protocol: TCP Source: Any Destination: Any Action: Allow
NSG1 connects to Subnet1. NSG2 connects to the network interface of VM2.
For each of the following statements, select Yes if the statement is true. Otherwise, select No.

Statements	Yes/No
From the internet you can connect to VM1 by using remote desktop	
From the internet, you can connect to VM2 by using remote desktop	
From VM1, you can connect to VM2 by using remote desktop.	

A. Mastered
B. Not Mastered
Answer: A

QUESTION 34
You have an Azure subscription that contains the following resources: 100 Azure virtual machines
20 Azure SQL databases 50 Azure file shares
You need to create a daily backup of all the resources by using Azure Backup. What is the minimum number of backup policies that you must create?

A. 1
B. 2
C. 3
D. 150
E. 170

Answer: C
QUESTION 35
- (4)
Note: This question is part of a series of questions that present the same scenario. Each question in the series contains a unique solution that might meet the stated goals. Some question sets might have more than one correct solution, while others might not have a correct solution.
After you answer a question in this section, you will NOT be able to return to it. As a result, these questions will not appear in the review screen.
You have an Azure subscription that contains the following users in an Azure Active Directory tenant named contoso.onmicrosoft.com:

Name	Role	Scope
Userl	Global administrator	Azure Active Directory
User2	Global administrator	Azure Active Directory
User3	User administrator	Azure Active Directory
User4	Owner	Azure Subscription

Userl creates a new Azure Active Directory tenant named external.contoso.onmicrosoft.com.
You need to create new user accounts in external.contoso.onmicrosoft.com.
Solution: You instruct User4 to create the user accounts. Does that meet the goal?
A. yes
B. No
Answer: B

QUESTION 36
(4)
You have an Azure subscription that includes data in following locations:

Name	Type
container1	Blob container
share1	Azure files share
DB1	SQL database
Table 1	Azure Table

You plan to export data by using Azure import/export job named Export1. You need to identify the data that can be exported by using Export1. Which data should you identify?

A. DB1
B. Table1
C. container1
D. Share1
Answer: C

QUESTION 37
-(4)
Note: This question is part of a series of questions that present the same scenario. Each question in the series contains a unique solution that might meet the stated goals. Some question sets might have more than one correct solution, while others might not have a correct solution. After you answer a question in this section, you will NOT be able to return to it. As a result, these questions will not appear in the review screen. You have an Azure subscription named Subscription1 that contains the resources shown in the following table.

Name	Type	Location	Resource group
RG1	Resource group	East US	Not applicable
RG2	Resource group	West Europe	Not applicable
RG3	Resource group	North Europe	Not applicable
VNET1	Virtual network	Central US	RG1
VM1	Virtual machine	West US	RG2

VM1 connects to a virtual network named VNET2 by using a network interface named NIC1. You need to create a new network interface named NIC2 for VM1. Solution: You create NIC2 in RG2 and West US. Does this meet the goal?

A. Yes
B. NO
Answer: A

QUESTION 38

-(4)
You have an Azure subscription.
Users access the resources in the subscription from either home or from customer sites. From home, users must establish a point to site VPN to access the Azure resources. The users on the customer sites access the Azure resources by using site to site VPNs.
You have a line of business app named App1 that runs on several Azure virtual machine. The virtual machines run Windows Server 2016. You need to ensure that the connections to App1 are spread across all the virtual machines.
What are two possible Azure services that you can use? Each correct answer presents a complete solution. NOTE: Each correct selection is worth one point.

A. a public load balancer
B. Traffic Manager
C. an Azure Content Delivery Network (CDN)
D. an internal load balancer
E. an Azure Application Gateway
Answer: D,E

QUESTION 39
-(4)
Note: This question is part of a series of questions that present the same scenario. Each question in the series contains a unique solution that might meet the stated goals. Some question sets might have more than one correct solution, while others might not have a correct solution.
After you answer a question in this section, you will NOT be able to return to it. As a result, these questions will not appear in the review screen.
You have an Azure Active Directory (Azure AD) tenant named Adatum and an Azure Subscription named Subscription1. Adatum contains a group named Developers. Subscription1 contains a resource group named Dev.
You need to provide the Developers group with the ability to create Azure logic apps in the Dev resource group. Solution: On Dev, you assign the Contributor role to the Developers group. Does this meet the goal?

A. Yes
B. No
Answer: A

QUESTION 40
-(2)
You need to resolve the licensing issue before you attempt to assign the license again. What should you do?

A. From the Groups blade, invite the user accounts to a new group.
B. From the Profile blade, modify the usage location.
C. From the Directory role blade, modify the directory role.
Answer: B

QUESTION 41

-

You have two subscriptions named Subscription1 and Subscription2. Each subscription is associated to a different Azure AD tenant.
Subscription1 contains a virtual network named VNet1.VNet1 contains an Azure virtual machine named VM1 and has an IP address space of 10.0.0.0/16. Subscription2 contains a virtual network named VNet2. VNet2 contains an Azure virtual machine named VM2 and has an IP address space of 10.10.0.0/24. You need to connect VNet1 to VNet2. What should you do first?

A. Move VNet1 to Subscription2.
B. Modify the IP address space of VNet2.
C. Provision virtual network gateways.
D. Move VM1 to Subscription2.
Answer: C

QUESTION 42

-

You have an on premises server that contains a folder named D:\Folder1.
You need to copy the contents of D:\Folder1 to the public container in an Azure Storage account named contoso data. Which command should you run?

A. https://contosodata.blob.core.windows.net/public
B. azcopy sync D:\folder1 https://contosodata.blob.core.windows.net/public snapshot
C. azcopy copy D:\folder1 https://contosodata.blob.core.windows.net/public recursive
D. az storage blob copy start batch D:\Folder1 https:// contosodata.blob.core.windows.net/public
Answer: C

QUESTION 43

-

Your on premises network contains an SMB share named Share1. You have an Azure subscription that contains the following resources: A web app named webapp1
A virtual network named VNET1
You need to ensure that webapp1 can connect to Share1. What should you deploy?

A. an Azure Application Gateway
B. an Azure Active Directory (Azure AD) Application Proxy
C. an Azure Virtual Network Gateway
Answer: C

QUESTION 44
You have an Azure Active Directory (Azure AD) domain that contains 5,000 user accounts. You create a new user account named AdminUser1. You need to assign the User administrator administrative role to AdminUser1. What should you do from the user account properties?
A. From the Directory role blade, modify the directory role.
B. From the Groups blade, invite the user account to a new group.
C. From the Licenses blade, assign a new license.

Answer: A
QUESTION 45
-
You have an Azure subscription that has a Recovery Services vault named Vault1. The subscription contains the virtual machines shown in the following table.

Name	Operating system	Auto shutdown
VM1	Windows Server 2012 R2	Off
VM2	Windows Server 2016	19:00
VM3	Ubuntu Server 18.04 LTS	Off
VM4	Windows 10	19:00

You plan to schedule backups to occur every night at 23:00. Which virtual machines can you back up by using Azure Backup?

A. VM1 only
B. VM1 and VM3 only
C. VM1. VM2, VM3andVM4
D. VM1 and VM2 only
Answer: C

QUESTION 46
-
You have an Azure Active Directory (Azure AD) tenant named contoso.onmicrosoft.com that contains 100 user accounts. You purchase 10 Azure AD Premium P2 licenses for the tenant. You need to ensure that 10 users can use all the Azure AD Premium features. What should you do?

A. From the Groups blade of each user, invite the users to a group.
B. From the Licenses blade of Azure AD, assign a license.
C. From the Directory role blade of each user, modify the directory role.
D. From the Azure AD domain, add an enterprise application.
Answer: B

QUESTION 47
-
You have an Azure subscription named Subscription1. Subscription1 contains two Azure virtual machines named VM1 and VM2. VM1 and VM2 run Windows Server 2016.
VM1 is backed up daily by Azure Backup without using the Azure Backup agent. VM1 is affected by ransomware that encrypts data. You need to restore the latest backup of VM1.
To which location can you restore the backup? To answer, select the appropriate options in the answer area. NOTE: Each correct selection is worth one point.

You can perform a file recovery of VM1 to:	VM1 only
	VM1 or a new Azure virtual machine only
	VM1 and VM2 only
	A new Azure virtual machine only
	Any Windows computer that has Internet connectivity
You can restore VM1 to:	VM1 only
	VM1 or a new Azure virtual machine only
	VM1 and VM2 only
	Any Windows computer that has Internet connectivity

A. Mastered
B. Not Mastered
Answer: A

QUESTION 48

-

You have an Azure subscription that contains an Azure virtual machine named VM1. VM1 runs a financial reporting app named App1 that does not support multiple active instances.
At the end of each month, CPU usage for VM1 peaks when App1 runs.
You need to create a scheduled runbook to increase the processor performance of VM1 at the end of each month. What task should you include in the runbook?

A. Add the Azure Performance Diagnostics agent to VM1.
B. Modify the VM size property of VM1.
C. Add VM1 to a scale set.
D. Increase the vCPU quota for the subscription.
E. Add a Desired State Configuration (DSC) extension to VM1.
Answer: B

QUESTION 49

-

You have the Azure virtual machines shown in the following table.

Name	Azure region
VM1	West Europe
VM2	West Europe
VM3	North Europe
VM4	North Europe

You have a Recovery Services vault that protects VM1 and VM2. You need to protect VM3 and VM4 by using Recovery Services. What should you do first?

A. Configure the extensions for VM3 and VM4.
B. Create a new Recovery Services vault.
C. Create a storage account.
D. Create a new backup policy.
Answer: B

QUESTION 50

-

You have an app named App1 that runs on an Azure web app named webapp1.
The developers at your company upload an update of App1 to a Git repository named GUI.
Webapp1 has the deployment slots shown in the following table.

Name	Function
Webapp1 prod	Production
Webapp1 test	Staging

You need to ensure that the App1 update is tested before the update is made available to users.
Which two actions should you perform? Each correct answer presents part of the solution.
NOTE Each correct selection is worth one point.

A. Stop webapp1 prod.
B. Stop webapp1 test
C. Deploy the App1 update to webapp1 test, and then test the update.
D. Deploy the App1 update to webapp1 prod, and then test the update.
E. Swap the slots.
Answer: CE

QUESTION 51

-

Note: This question is part of a series of questions that present the same scenario. Each question in the series contains a unique solution that might meet the stated goals. Some question sets might have more than one correct solution, while others might not have a correct solution.
After you answer a question in this section, you will NOT be able to return to it. As a result, these questions will not appear in the review screen. You have an Azure subscription that contains 10 virtual networks. The virtual networks are hosted in separate resource groups.
Another administrator plans to create several network security groups (NSGs) in the subscription.
You need to ensure that when an NSG is created, it automatically blocks TCP port 8080 between the virtual networks. Solution: You assign a built in policy definition to the subscription. Does this meet the goal?

A. Yes
B. No
Answer: B

QUESTION 52

-

You have an Azure subscription.
You plan to use Azure Resource Manager templates to deploy 50 Azure virtual machines that will be part of the same availability set. You need to ensure that as many virtual machines as possible are available if the fabric fails or during servicing.
How should you configure the template? To answer, select the appropriate options in the answer area. NOTE: Each correct selection is worth one point.

```
"Sschema": https://scheaa.managezent.azu:e.cca/scheaas/20iS  Oi  Oi/depioyaent>4iate.json,
"contentversion" : : "1.0.0.0",
"parameters" :{},
Resources : {
        {

"type": "Microsoft .Compute/avaiiabflitySets",
"name": "ha",
"apiversion." : "2017  12  01",
                "properties": {
                        "platformFaultDomainCount":

                        "platformUpdateDomainCount":
                        }
                    }
                }
            }
```

A. Mastered
B. Not Mastered
Answer: A

QUESTION 53

-

You have an Azure Active Directory (Azure AD) tenant.
You need to create a conditional access policy that requires all users to use multi factor authentication when they access the Azure portal. Which three settings should you configure?

A. Mastered
B. Not Mastered
Answer: A

QUESTION 54

-

You recently created a new Azure subscription that contains a user named Admin1.
Admin1 attempts to deploy an Azure Marketplace resource by using an Azure Resource Manager template.
Admin1 deploys the template by using Azure PowerShell and receives the following error message: "User failed validation to purchase resources. Error message: "Legal terms have not been accepted for this item on this subscription.
To accept legal terms, please go to the Azure portal (http://go.microsoft.com/fwlink/?LinkI d=534873) and configure programmatic deployment for the Marketplace item or create it there for the first time." You need to ensure that Admin1 can deploy the Marketplace resource successfully. What should you do?

A. From Azure PowerShell, run the Set AzApiManagementSubscription cmdlet
B. From the Azure portal, register the Microsoft.Marketplace resource provider

C. From Azure PowerShell, run the Set AzMarketplaceTerms cmdlet
D. From the Azure portal, assign the Billing administrator role to Admin1
Answer: C

QUESTION 55

-

You have an Azure tenant that contains two subscriptions named Subscription1 and Subscription2.
In Subscription1, you deploy a virtual machine named Server1 that runs Windows Server 2016. Server1 uses managed disks. You need to move Server1 to Subscription2. The solution must minimize administration effort. What should you do first?

A. In Subscription2, create a copy of the virtual disk.
B. From Azure PowerShell, run the Move AzureRmResource cmdlet.
C. Create a snapshot of the virtual disk.
D. Create a new virtual machine in Subscription2.
Answer: B

QUESTION 55

-

You have an Azure App Service plan that hosts an Azure App Service named App1. You configure one production slot and four staging slots for App1. You need to allocate 10 percent of the traffic to each staging slot and 60 percent of the traffic to the production slot.
What should you add to Appl1?

A. slots to the Testing in production blade
B. a performance test
C. a WebJob
D. templates to the Automation script blade
Answer: A

QUESTION 56

-

You are creating an Azure load balancer.
You need to add an IPv6 load balancing rule to the load balancer.
How should you complete the Azure PowerShell script?

A. Mastered
B. Not Mastered
Answer: A

QUESTION 57

-

Note: This question is part of a series of questions that present the same scenario. Each question in the series contains a unique solution that might meet the stated goals. Some question sets might have more than one correct solution, while others might not have a correct solution.

After you answer a question in this section, you will NOT be able to return to it. As a result, these questions will not appear in the review screen. You have an Azure web app named Appl. App1 runs in an Azure App Service plan named Plan1. Plan1 is associated to the Free pricing tier.

You discover that App1 stops each day after running continuously for 60 minutes. You need to ensure that App1 can run continuously for the entire day. Solution: You change the pricing tier of Plan1 to Basic. Does this meet the goal?

A. Yes
B. No
Answer: A

QUESTION 58

-

You have a deployment template named Template1 that is used to deploy 10 Azure web apps. You need to identify what to deploy before you deploy Template1. The solution must minimize Azure costs. What should you identify?

A. 10 App Service plans
B. one Azure Traffic Manager
C. five Azure Application Gateways
D. one App Service plan
E. one Azure Application Gateway
Answer: D

QUESTION 59

-

You need to deploy two Azure web apps named WebApp1 and WebApp2. The web apps have the following requirements: WebApp1
must be able to use staging slots
WebApp2 must be able to access the resources located on an Azure virtual network
What is the least costly plan that you can use to deploy each web app? To answer, select the appropriate options in the answer area. NOTE: Each correct selection is worth one point.

WebApp1	D1 Dev/Test
	F1 Dev/Test
	I1 Production
	P3 Production

WebApp2	S1 Production
	D1 Dev/Test
	F1 Dev/Test
	I1 Production
	P3 Production
	S1 Production

A. Mastered
B. Not Mastered
Answer: A

QUESTION 60

-

You have an Azure Storage account named storage1.
You have an Azure App Service app named app1 and an app named App2 that runs in an Azure container instance. Each app uses a managed identity. You need to ensure that App1 and App2 can read blobs from storage1 for the next 30 days. What should you configure in storage1 for each app?

App1:	Access keys
	Advanced security
	Access control (IAM)
	Shared access signatures (SAS)

App2:	Access keys
	Advanced security
	Access control (IAM)
	Shared access signatures (SAS)

A. Mastered
B. Not Mastered
Answer: A

QUESTION 61

-

You have a service deployed to a Kubernetes cluster.
Another application needs to access the service via the private IP address of the pod.Which of the following would you define as the networking type for the cluster to meet this requirement?
A. Kubenet
B. Azure container networking plugin
C. Service Endpoints
D. Network security groups
Answer: B

QUESTION 62

-

You have an Azure subscription that contains the resources shown in the following table.

Name	Type
Cluster 1	Azure Kubernetes Service (AKS)
Registry 1	Azure container Registry
Application1	Container image

You need to deploy Application1 to Cluster1. Which command should you run?
A. az acr build
B. az aks create
C. docker build
D. kubectl apply
Answer: A

QUESTION 63
-
You have an Azure subscription that contains the resources shown in the following table.

Name	Type	Region
RG1	Resource group	West US
RG2	Resource group	East Asia
storage1	Storage account	West US
storage2	Storage account	East Asia
VM1	Virtual machine	West US
VNET1	Virtual network	West US
VNET2	Virtual network	East Asia

VM1 connects to VNET1.
You need to connect VM1 to VNET2.
Solution: You create a new network interface, and then you add the network interface to VM1.
Does this meet the goal?
A. Yes
B. No
Answer: B

QUESTION 64
You have an Azure Active Directory (Azure AD) tenant named Tenant1 and an Azure subscription named You enable Azure AD Privileged Identity Management. You need to secure the members of the Lab Creator role. The solution must ensure that the lab creators request access when they create labs.
What should you do first?
A. From Azure AD Privileged Identity Management, edit the role settings for Lab Creator.
B. From Subscription1 edit the members of the Lab Creator role.
C. From Azure AD Identity Protection, creates a user risk policy.
D. From Azure AD Privileged Identity Management, discover the Azure resources of Conscription.
Answer: A

QUESTION 65
-
You create an Azure Migrate project named TestMig in a resource group named test migration.
You need to discover which on premises virtual machines to assess for migration.
Which three actions should you perform in sequence? To answer, select the appropriate actions from the list of actions to the answer area and arrange them in the correct order.

Answer Area
Configure the collector and start discovery
Create a migration group in the project
Create a collector virtual machine
Create an assessment in the project
Download the OVA file for the collector appliance

A. Mastered
B. Not Mastered
Answer: A

QUESTION 66

-

You have an Azure subscription named Subscription1 that contains an Azure virtual network named VM1. VM1 is in a resource group named RG1. VM1 runs services that will be used to deploy resources to RG1.
You need to ensure that a service running on VM1 can manage the resources in RG1 by using the identity of VM1. What should you do first?

A. From the Azure portal modify the Access control (1AM) settings of VM1.
B. From the Azure portal, modify the Policies settings of RG1.
C. From the Azure portal, modify the value of the Managed Service Identity option for VM1.
D. From the Azure portal, modify the Access control (IAM) settings of RG1.
Answer: C

QUESTION 67

-

Note This question is part of a series of questions that present the same seer Some question sets might have more than one correct solution, while others might not have a correct solution.
After you answer a question in this section, you will NOT be able to return to it. As a result, these questions will not appear in the review screen.
You manage a virtual network named VNet1 that is hosted in the West US Azure region. VNet1 hosts two virtual machines named VM1 and VM2 that run Windows Server.
You need to inspect all the network traffic from VM1 to VM2 for a period of three hours.
Solution: From Performance Monitor, you create a Data Collector Set (DCS)
Does this meet the goal?

A. Yes
B. No
Answer: B

QUESTION 68

-

You manage a virtual network named VNet1 that is hosted in the West US region. Two virtual machines named VM1 and VM2, both running Windows Server, are on VNet1. You need to monitor traffic between
VM1 and VM2 for a period of five hours.
As a solution, you propose to create a connection monitor in Azure Network Watcher. Does this solution meet the goal?

A. Yes
B. No
Answer: A

QUESTION 69

-

Your company has a main office in London that contains 100 client computers. Three years ago, you migrated to Azure Active Directory (Azure AD). The company's security policy states that all personal devices and corporate owned devices must be registered or joined to Azure AD.
A remote user named User1 is unable to join a personal device to Azure AD from a home network. You verify that other users can join their devices to Azure AD. You need to ensure that User1 can join the device to Azure AD. What should you do?

A. From the Device settings blade, modify the Users may join devices to Azure AD setting.
B. From the Device settings blade, modify the Maximum number of devices per user setting.
C. Create a point to site VPN from the home network of User1 to Azure.
D. Assign the User administrator role to User1.
Answer: B

QUESTION 70

-

A web developer creates a web application that you plan to deploy as an Azure web app. Users must enter credentials to access the web application. You create a new web app named WebApp1 and deploy the web application to WebApp1. You need to disable anonymous access to WebApp1.
What should you configure?

A. Access control (IAM)
B. Advanced Tools
C. Deployment credentials
D. Authentication/Authorization
Answer: D

QUESTION 71

-

You are deploying a containerized web application in Azure.

When deploying the web app, which of the following are valid container image sources?

A. Virtual machine
B. Docker hub
C. ACR
D. On premises
Answer: BC

QUESTION 72

-

You deploy a load balancer that has the following configurations:

- NameLB1
- Type: internal
- SKU: Standard
- Virtual network: VNET1

You need to ensure that you can add VM1 and VM2 to the backend pool of LB1. Solution: You disassociate the public IP address from the network interface of VM2.
Does this meet the goal?

A. Yes
B. No
Answer: B

QUESTION 73

-

Note: This question is part of a series of questions that present the same scenario. Each question in the series contains a unique solution that might meet the stated goals. Some question sets might have more than one correct solution, while others might not have a correct solution. After you answer a question in this section, you will NOT be able to return to it. As a result, these questions will not appear in the review screen. Your company has 100 users located in an office in Paris.
The on premises network contains the servers shown in the following table.

Name	Operating system	Configuration
Server1	Windows Server 2012 R2	Microsoft Exchange Server 2016
Server2	Windows Server 2016	Microsoft SQL Server 2016
Server3	Windows Server 2016	Domain controller
Server4	Red Hat Enterprise Linux	File server

You create a new subscription. You need to move all the servers to Azure. Solution: You use Azure Site Recovery. Does this meet the goal?

A. Yes
B. No

Answer: A

QUESTION 74

-

You have an Azure Resource Manager template named Template1 that is used to deploy an Azure virtual machine.

Template1 contains the following text:
"location": {
"type": "String",
"defaultValue": "eastus",
"allowedValues": [
"canadacentral",
"eastus",
"westeurope",
"westus"]
}

The variables section in Template1 contains the following text: "location": "westeurope" The resources section in Template1 contains the following text:
"type": "Microsoft.Compute/virtualMachines",
"apiVersion": "2018 10 01",
"name": "[variables('vmName')]",
"location": 'Westeurope",
You need to deploy the virtual machine to the West US location by using Template1. What should you do?

A. Modify the location in the resource section to westus
B. Select West US during the deployment
C. Modify the location in the variables section to westus

Answer: A
QUESTION 75

-

You are troubleshooting a performance issue for an Azure Application Gateway.
You need to compare the total requests to the failed requests during the past six hours. What should you use?

A. Metrics in Application Gateway
B. Diagnostics logs in Application Gateway
C. NSG flow logs in Azure Network Watcher
D. Connection monitor in Azure Network Watcher

Answer: A

Chapter 2: Practice Questions &Answers Part 2

QUESTION 76

-

You have an Azure Kubernetes Service (AKS) cluster named AKS1 and a computer named Computer1 that runs Windows 10. Computer1 that has the Azure CLI installed.
You need to install the kubectl client on Computer1.
Which command should you run? Mastered
A. Not Mastered

Answer: A
QUESTION 77

-

You have an Azure subscription that contains the resources shown in the following table.

Name	Type	Region
RG1	Resource group	West US
RG2	Resource group	East Asia
storage1	Storage account	West US
storage2	Storage account	East Asia
VM1	Virtual machine	West US
VNET1	Virtual network	West US
VNET2	Virtual network	East Asia

VM1 connects to VNET1.
You need to connect VM1 to VNET2.
Solution: You delete VM1. You recreate VM1, and then you create a new network interface for VM1 and connect it to VNET2. Does this meet the goal?

A. Yes
B. No

Answer: B
QUESTION 78

-

You need to create an Azure virtual machine named VM1 that requires a static private IP address configured inside the IP address space for the VNet in which the VM resides. How do you configure a static IP address for this Azure VM?

A. After the VM has been created, create a new network interface and configure a static IP address for that network interface
B. When creating a VM in the portal, select New next to private ip address and choose static after assigning the correct IP address
C. When creating the VM in the portal, change the setting from dynamic to static on the networking tab under private IP address

D. After the VM has been created, go to the network interface attached to the VM and change the IP configuration to static assignment

Answer: D
QUESTION 79
-
You have an Azure subscription that contains two virtual machines as shown in the following table.

Name	Operating system	Location	IP addresses	DNS server
VM1	Windows server 2019	West Europe	10.0.0.4	Default (Azure provides)
VM2	Windows server 2019	West Europe	10.0.0.5	Default (Azure provides)

You perform a reverse DNS lookup for 10.0.0.4 from VM2. Which FQDN will be returned?

A. vm1.core.windows.net
B. vm1.internal.cloudapp.net
C. vm1.westeurope.cloudapp.azure.com
D. vm1.azure.com

Answer: D
QUESTION 80
You plan to migrate an on premises Hyper V environment to Azure by using Azure Site Recovery. The Hyper V environment is managed by using Microsoft System Center Virtual Machine Manager (VMM).
The Hyper V environment contains the virtual machines in the following table.

Name	Operating system	OS disk size	BitLockerDrive Encryption enabled on OS disks	Generation
DC1	Windows server 2016	500GB	No	2
FS1	UBUNTU 16.04 LTS	200GB	No	2
CA1	Windows server 2012 R2	1TB	Yes	1
SQL1	Windows server 2016	200GB	No	2

Which virtual machine can be migrated by using Azure Site Recovery?

A. DC1
B. FS1
C. CA1
D. SQL1

Answer: D

QUESTION 81
You have an Azure subscription that contains a virtual machine named VM1. VM1 hosts a line of business application that is available 24 hours a day. VM1 has one network interface and one managed disk. VM1 uses the D4s v3 size.
You plan to make the following changes to VM1: Change the size to D8s v3.
Add a 500 GB managed disk. Add the Puppet Agent extension.
Attach an additional network interface. Which change will cause downtime for VM1?

A. Add a 500 GB managed disk.
B. Attach an additional network interface.
C. Add the Puppet Agent extension.
D. Change the size to D8s v3.

Answer: D
QUESTION 82
You are the global administrator for an Azure Active Directory (Azure AD) tenant named adatum.com. You need to enable two step verification for Azure users. What should you do?

A. Configure a playbook in Azure AD conditional access policy.
B. Create an Azure AD conditional access policy.
C. Create and configure the Identify Hub.
D. Install and configure Azure AD Connect.

Answer: B
QUESTION 83
-
You have an Azure subscription that contains a virtual network named VNet1. VNet 1 has two subnets named Subnet1 and Subnet2. VNet1 is in the West Europe Azure region.
The subscription contains the virtual machines in the following table.

Name	Connected to
VM1	Subnet1
VM2	Subnet1
VM3	Subnet2

You need to deploy an application gateway named AppGW1 to VNet1. What should you do first?

A. Add a service endpoint.
B. Add a virtual network.
C. Move VM3 to Subnet1.
D. Stop VM1 and VM2.

Answer: D

QUESTION 84

-

You have an Azure subscription that contains an Azure Service Bus named Bus1.
Your company plans to deploy two Azure web apps named App1 and App2. The web apps will create messages that have the following
requirements: Each message created by App1 must be consumed by only a single consumer
Each message created by App2 will be consumed by multiple consumers.
Which resource should you create for each web app?

A. Mastered
B. Not Mastered

Answer: A

QUESTION 85

-

Note: This question is part of a series of questions that present the same scenario. Each question in the series contains a unique solution that might meet the stated goals. Some question sets might have more than one correct solution, while others might not have a correct solution. After you answer a question in this section, you will NOT be able to return to it. As a result, these questions will not appear in the review screen. You have an Azure web app named App1. App1 runs in an Azure App Service plan named Plan1. Plan1 is associated to the Free pricing tier.
You discover that App1 stops each day after running continuously for 60 minutes. You need to ensure that App1 can run continuously for the entire day. Solution: You add a continuous WebJob to App1. Does this meet the goal?

A. Yes
B. No

Answer: B

QUESTION 86

-

Note: This question is part of a series of questions that present the same scenario. Each question in the series contains a unique solution that might meet the stated goals. Some question sets might have more than one correct solution, while others might not have a correct solution. After you answer a question in this section, you will NOT be able to return to it. As a result, these questions will not appear in the review screen. Your company has 100 users located in an office in Paris.
The on premises network contains the servers shown in the following table.

Name	Operating system	Configuration
Server1	Windows Server 2012 R2	Microsoft Exchange Server 2016
Server2	Windows Server 2016	Microsoft SQL Server 2016
Server3	Windows Server 2016	Domain controller
Server4	Red Hat enterprise Linux 7.5	File server

You create a new subscription. You need to move all the servers to Azure. Solution: You run azcopy.exe. Does this meet the goal?

A. Yes
B. No

Answer: B
QUESTION 87
-
You onboard 10 Azure virtual machines to Azure Automation State Configuration.
You need to use Azure Automation State Configuration to manage the ongoing consistency of the virtual machine configurations.
Which three actions should you perform in sequence? To answer, move the appropriate actions from the list of actions to the answer area and arrange them in the correct order.
NOTE: More than one order of answer choices is correct. You will receive credit for any of the correct orders you select.

Actions	Answer Area
Assign tags to the virtual machines	
Check the compliance status of the node	
Compile a configure into a node configuration	
Upload a configuration to Azure Automation state configuration.	
Create a management group	

A. Mastered
B. Not Mastered

Answer: A
QUESTION 88
-
You have an Azure Active Directory (Azure AD) tenant that has Azure AD Privileged Identity Management configured.

You have 10 users who are assigned the Security Administrator role for the tenant. You need the users to verify whether they still require the Security Administrator role. What should you do?

A. From Azure AD Identity Protection, configure a user risk policy.
B. From Azure AD Privileged Identity Management, create an access review.
C. From Azure AD Identity Protection, configure the Weekly Digest.
D. From Azure AD Privileged Identity Management, create a conditional access policy.

Answer: B
QUESTION 89

-

You have an Azure Active Directory (Azure AD) tenant.
All administrators must enter a verification code to access the Azure portal.
You need to ensure that the administrators can access the Azure portal only from your on premises network. What should you configure?

A. an Azure AD Identity Protection user risk policy.
B. the multi factor authentication service settings.
C. the default for all the roles in Azure AD Privileged Identity Management
D. an Azure AD Identity Protection sign in risk policy

Answer: B
QUESTION 90

-

You have an on premises network that contains a Hyper V host named Host1. Host1 runs Windows Server 2016 and hosts 10 virtual machines that run Windows Server 2016.
You plan to replicate the virtual machines to Azure by using Azure Site Recovery. You create a Recovery Services vault named ASR1 and a Hyper V site named Site1. You need to add Host1 to ASR1.
What should you do?

A. Download the installation file for the Azure Site Recovery Provider.Download the vault registration key.Install the Azure Site Recovery Provider on Host1 and register the server.
B. Download the installation file for the Azure Site Recovery Provider.Download the storage account key.Install the Azure Site Recovery Provider on Host1 and register the server.
C. Download the installation file for the Azure Site Recovery Provider.Download the vault registration key.Install the Azure Site Recovery Provider on each virtual machine and register the virtual machines.
D. Download the installation file for the Azure Site Recovery Provider.Download the storage account key.Install the Azure Site Recovery Provider on each virtual machine and register the virtual machines.

Answer: A
QUESTION 91

You need to meet the technical requirement for VM4. What should you create and configure?

A. an Azure Notification Hub
B. an Azure Event Hub
C. an Azure Logic App
D. an Azure services Bus

Answer: B
QUESTION 92
- (2)
You need to prepare the environment to meet the authentication requirements.
Which two actions should you perform? Each correct answer presents part of the solution.
NOTE: Each correct selection is worth one point.

A. Allow inbound TCP port 8080 to the domain controllers in the Miami office.
B. Addhttp://autogon.microsoftazuread sso.com to the intranet zone of each client computer in the Miami office.
C. Join the client computers in the Miami office to Azure AD.
D. Install the Active Directory Federation Services (AD FS) role on a domain controller in the Miami office.
E. Install Azure AD Connect on a server in the Miami office and enable Pass through Authentication.

Answer: BE
QUESTION 93
- (4)
Note: This question is part of a series of questions that present the same scenario. Each question in the series contains a unique solution that might meet the stated goals. Some question sets might have more than one correct solution, while others might not have a correct solution.
After you answer a question in this section, you will NOT be able to return to it. As a result, these questions will not appear in the review screen.
You have an Azure Active Directory (Azure AD) tenant named Adatum and an Azure Subscription named Subscription1. Adatum contains a group named Developers. Subscription1 contains a resource group named Dev.
You need to provide the Developers group with the ability to create Azure logic apps in the Dev resource group. Solution: On Subscription1, you assign the DevTest Labs User role to the Developers group. Does this meet the goal?

A. Yes
B. No

Answer: B
QUESTION 94

You have an Azure Active Directory (Azure AD) tenant named adatum.com that contains the users shown in the following table.

Name	Role
User	None
User2	Global administer
User3	Cloud device administrator
User4	Intune administrator

Adatum.com has the following configurations: Users may join devices to Azure AD is set to User1. Additional local administrators on Azure AD joined devices is set to None.
You deploy Windows 10 to a computer named Computer. User1 joins Computer1 to adatum.com. You need to identify which users are added to the local Administrators group on Computer1.

A. User1 only
B. User1, User2, and User3 only
C. User1 and User2 only
D. User1, User2, User3, and User4
E. User2 only

Answer: C
QUESTION 95
-(4)
You have an Azure subscription that contains an Azure Active Directory (Azure AD) tenant named adatum.com. The tenant contains 500 user accounts.
You deploy Microsoft Office 365. You configure Office 365 to use the user accounts in adatum.com. You configure 60 users to connect to mailboxes in Microsoft Exchange Online.
You need to ensure that the 60 users use Azure Multi Factor Authentication (MFA) to connect to the Exchange Online mailboxes. The solution must only affect connections to the Exchange Online mailboxes.
What should you do?

A. From the multi factor authentication page, configure the Multi Factor Auth status for each user
B. From Azure Active Directory admin center, create a conditional access policy
C. From the multi factor authentication page, modify the verification options
D. From the Azure Active Directory admin center, configure an authentication method

Answer: A
QUESTION 96
- (4)
You have an Azure subscription named Subscription1.
You have 5 TB of data that you need to transfer to Subscription1. You plan to use an Azure Import/Export job. What can you use as the destination of the imported data?

A. Azure Data Lake Store
B. a virtual machine
C. the Azure File Sync Storage Sync Service
D. Azure Blob storage

Answer: D
QUESTION 97
-(4)
You have an Azure subscription that contains the resources shown in the following table.

Name	Type	Location
VNET1	Virtual network	East US
IP1	Public IP address	West Europe
RTI	Route table	North Europe

You need to create a network interface named NIC1. In which location can you create NIC1?

A. East US and North Europe only.
B. East US and West Europe only.
C. East US, West Europe, and North Europe.
D. East US only.

Answer: D
QUESTION 98
-(4)
Note: This question is part of a series of questions that present the same scenario. Each question in the series contains a unique solution that might meet the stated goals. Some question sets might have more than one correct solution, while others might not have a correct solution. After you answer a question in this section, you will NOT be able to return to it. As a result, these questions will not appear in the review screen. You have an Azure subscription that contains the following resources:
A virtual network that has a subnet named Subnet1
Two network security groups (NSGs) named NSG VM1 and NSG Subnet1
A virtual machine named VM1 that has the required Windows Server configurations to allow Remote Desktop connections NSG Subnet1 has the default inbound security rules only.
NSG VM1 has the default inbound security rules and the following custom inbound security rule: Priority: 100
Source: Any
Source port range: * Destination: *
Destination port range: 3389 Protocol: UDP
Action: Allow
VM1 connects to Subnet1. NSG1 VM1 is associated to the network interface of VM1. NSG Subnet1 is associated to Subnet1. You need to be able to establish Remote Desktop connections from the internet to VM1.

Solution: You add an inbound security rule to NSG Subnet1 that allows connections from the Any source to the Virtual Network destination for port range 3389 and uses the TCP protocol. You remove NSG VM1 from the network interface of VM1.
Does this meet the goal?

A. Yes
B. No

Answer: B
QUESTION 99
- (4)
You have an Azure Active Directory (Azure AD) tenant named contosocloud.onmicrosoft.com.
Your company has a public DNS zone for contoso.com.
You add contoso.com as a custom domain name to Azure AD. You need to ensure that Azure can verify the domain name. Which type of DNS record should you create?

A. PTR
B. MX
C. NSEC3
D. RRSIG

Answer: B
QUESTION 100
- (4)
You plan to use the Azure Import/Export service to copy files to a storage account.
Which two files should you create before you prepare the drives for the import job? Each correct answer presents part of the solution. NOTE: Each correct selection is worth one point.

A. an XML manifest file
B. a driveset CSV file
C. a dataset CSV file
D. a PowerShell PS1 file
E. a JSON configuration file

Answer: BC
QUESTION 101
- (4)
You have an Azure subscription that contains the following users in an Azure Active Directory tenant named contoso.onmicrosoft.com:

Name	Role	Scope
User1	Global administrator	Azure Active Directory
User2	Global administrator	Azure Active Directory
User3	User administrator	Azure Active Directory
User4	Owner	Azure Subscription

User1 creates a new Azure Active Directory tenant named external.contoso.onmicrosoft.com.
You need to create new user accounts in external.contoso.com.onmicrosoft.com.
Solution: You instruct User2 to create the user accounts.

A. Yes
B. No

Answer: A
QUESTION 102
-(4)
You have an Azure virtual machine named VM1.
The network interface for VM1 is configured as shown in the exhibit. (Click the Exhibit tab.)
You deploy a web server on VM1, and then create a secure website that is accessible by using the HTTPS protocol VM1 is used as a web server only.
You need to ensure that users can connect to the website from the Internet. What should you do?

A. Change the priority of Rule3 to 450.
B. Change the priority of Rule6 to 100
C. DeleteRule1.
D. Create a new inbound rule that allows TCP protocol 443 and configure the protocol to have a priority of 501.

Answer: D
QUESTION 103
-(4)
You have two Azure virtual machines named VM1 and VM2. You have two Recovery Services vaults named RSV1 and RSV2. VM2 is protected by RSV1.
You need to use RSV2 to protect VM2. What should you do first?

A. From the RSV1 blade, click Backup items and stop the VM2 backup.
B. From the RSV1 blade, click Backup Jobs and export the VM2 backup.
C. From the RSV1 blade, click Backu
D. From the Backup blade, select the backup for the virtual machine, and then click Backup.
E. From the VM2 blade, click Disaster recovery, click Replication settings, and then select RSV2 as the Recovery Services vault.

Answer: D
QUESTION 104

-(4)
You have an Azure Active Directory (Azure AD) tenant named contoso.com. Multi factor authentication (MFA) is enabled for all users. You need to provide users with the ability to bypass MFA for 10 days on devices to which they have successfully signed in by using MFA. What should you do?

A. From the multi factor authentication page, configure the users' settings.
B. From Azure AD, create a conditional access policy.
C. From the multi factor authentication page, configure the service settings.
D. From the MFA blade in Azure AD, configure the MFA Server settings.

Answer: C
QUESTION 105
-(4)
Note: This question is part of a series of questions that present the same scenario. Each question in the series contains a unique solution that might meet the stated goals. Some question sets might have more than one correct solution, while others might not have a correct solution. After you answer a question in this section, you will NOT be able to return to it. As a result, these questions will not appear in the review screen. You have an Azure subscription that contains the following resources:
A virtual network that has a subnet named Subnet1
Two network security groups (NSGs) named NSG VM1 and NSG Subnet1
A virtual machine named VM1 that has the required Windows Server configurations to allow Remote Desktop connections NSG Subnet1 has the default inbound security rules only.
NSG VM1 has the default inbound security rules and the following custom inbound security rule: Priority: 100
Source: Any
Source port range: * Destination: *
Destination port range: 3389
Protocol: UDP Action: Allow
VM1 connects to Subnet1. NSG1 VM1 is associated to the network interface of VM1. NSG Subnet1 is associated to
Subnet1. You need to be able to establish Remote Desktop connections from the internet to VM1. Solution: You modify the custom rule for NSG VM1 to use the internet as a source and TCP as a protocol. Does this meet the goal?

A. Yes
B. No

Answer: A
QUESTION 106
-(4)
Note: This question is part of a series of questions that present the same scenario. Each question in the series contains a unique solution that might meet the stated goals. Some question sets might have more than one correct solution, while others might not have a correct solution.

After you answer a question in this section, you will NOT be able to return to it. As a result, these questions will not appear in the review screen.
You have a computer named Computer1 that has a point to site VPN connection to an Azure virtual network named VNet1. The point to site connection uses a self signed certificate.
From Azure, you download and install the VPN client configuration package on a computer named Computer2.
You need to ensure that you can establish a point to site VPN connection to VNet1 from Computer2. Solution: You modify the Azure Active Directory (Azure AD) authentication policies.
Does this meet this goal?

A. Yes
B. No

Answer: B
QUESTION 107
-(4)
Note: This question is part of a series of questions that present the same scenario. Each question in the series contains a unique solution that might meet the stated goals. Some question sets might have more than one correct solution, while others might not have a correct solution.
After you answer a question in this section, you will NOT be able to return to it. As a result, these questions will not appear in the review screen. You have an Azure virtual machine named VM1 that runs Windows Server 2016.
You need to create an alert in Azure when more than two error events are logged to the System log on VM1 within an hour. Solution: You create an event subscription on VM1. You create an alert in Azure Monitor and specify VM1 as the source.
Does this meet the goal?
A. Yes
B. No

Answer: B
QUESTION 108
-(4)
You have an Azure subscription.
Users access the resources in the subscription from either home or from customer sites. From home, users must establish a point to site VPN to access the Azure resources. The users on the customer sites access the Azure resources by using site to site VPNs.
You have a line of business app named App1 that runs on several Azure virtual machine. The virtual machines run Windows Server 2016. You need to ensure that the connections to App1 are spread across all the virtual machines.
What are two possible Azure services that you can use? Each correct answer presents a complete solution. NOTE: Each correct selection is worth one point.

A. a public load balancer
B. Traffic Manager
C. an Azure Content Delivery Network (CDN)

D. an internal load balancer
E. an Azure Application Gateway

Answer: DE
QUESTION 109
-(4)
Your on premises network contains an Active Directory domain named adatum.com that is synced to Azure Active Directory (Azure AD). Password writeback is disabled.
In adatum.com, you create the users shown in the following table.

Name	Account option
User1	User must change password at next logon.
User2	Store password by using reversible encryption.
User3	A smart card is required for interactive logon.

Which users must sign in from a computer joined to adatum.com?

A. User2 only
B. User1 and User3 only
C. User1, User2, and User3
D. User2 and User3 only
E. User1 only
Answer: E
QUESTION 110
You have an Azure subscription that contains the following users in an Azure Active Directory tenant named contoso.onmicrosoft.com:

Name	Role	Scope
User1	Global administrator	Azure Active Directory
User2	Global administrator	Azure Active Directory
User3	User administrator	Azure Active Directory
User4	Owner	Azure Subscription

User1 creates a new Azure Active Directory tenant named external.contoso.onmicrosoft.com.
You need to create new user accounts in external.contoso.com.onmicrosoft.com.
Solution: You instruct User3 to create the user accounts.

A. Yes
B. No

Answer: B
QUESTION 111

You need to meet the technical requirement for VM4. What should you create and configure?

A. an Azure Notification Hub
B. an Azure Event Hub
C. an Azure Logic App
D. an Azure services Bus

Answer: B
QUESTION 112
-(2)
You need to prepare the environment to meet the authentication requirements.
Which two actions should you perform? Each correct answer presents part of the solution.
NOTE: Each correct selection is worth one point.

A. Allow inbound TCP port 8080 to the domain controllers in the Miami office.
B. Addhttp://autogon.microsoftazuread sso.com to the intranet zone of each client computer in the Miami office.
C. Join the client computers in the Miami office to Azure AD.
D. Install the Active Directory Federation Services (AD FS) role on a domain controller in the Miami office.
E. Install Azure AD Connect on a server in the Miami office and enable Pass through Authentication.

Answer: BE
QUESTION 113
-(2)
You need to resolve the licensing issue before you attempt to assign the license again. What should you do?

A. From the Groups blade, invite the user accounts to a new group.
B. From the Profile blade, modify the usage location.
C. From the Directory role blade, modify the directory role.

Answer: A
QUESTION 114
-(2)
Which blade should you instruct the finance department auditors to use?

A. invoices
B. partner information

C. cost analysis
D. External services

Answer: A
QUESTION 115
-(2)
You need to resolve the Active Directory issue. What should you do?

A. From Active Directory Users and Computers, select the user accounts, and then modify the User Principal Name value.
B. Run idfix.exe, and then use the Edit action.
C. From Active Directory Domains and Trusts, modify the list of UPN suffixes.
D. From Azure AD Connect, modify the outbound synchronization rule.

Answer: B
QUESTION 116
-(4)
Note: This question is part of a series of questions that present the same scenario. Each question in the series contains a unique solution that might meet the stated goals. Some question sets might have more than one correct solution, while others might not have a correct solution.
After you answer a question in this section, you will NOT be able to return to it. As a result, these questions will not appear in the review screen.
You have a computer named Computer1 that has a point to site VPN connection to an Azure virtual network named VNet1. The point to site connection uses a self signed certificate.
From Azure, you download and install the VPN client configuration package on a computer named Computer2.
You need to ensure that you can establish a point to site VPN connection to VNet1 from Computer2. Solution: On Computer2, you set the Startup type for the IPSec Policy Agent service to Automatic.
Does this meet the goal?

A. Yes
B. No

Answer: B
QUESTION 117
You have an Azure Active Directory (Azure AD) tenant named adatum.com that contains the users shown in the following table.

Name	Role
User1	None
User2	Global administrator
User3	Cloud device administrator
User4	Intune adminstrator

Adatum.com has the following configurations: Users may join devices to Azure AD is set to User1. Additional local administrators on Azure AD joined devices is set to None.
You deploy Windows 10 to a computer named Computer. User1 joins Computer1 to adatum.com. You need to identify which users are added to the local Administrators group on Computer1.

A. User1 only
B. User1, User2, and User3 only
C. User1 and User2 only
D. User1, User2, User3, and User4
E. User2 only

Answer: C
QUESTION 118
-(4)
You have an Azure virtual machine named VM1 that runs Windows Server 2019. You sign in to VM1 as a user named User 1 and perform the following actions:
* Create files on drive C.
* Create files on drive 0.
* Modify the screen saver timeout.
* Change the desktop background. You plan to redeploy VM1. Which changes will be lost after you redeploy VM1?

A. the modified screen saver timeout
B. the new desktop background
C. the new files on drive
D. The new files on drive C

Answer: D
QUESTION 119
-(4)
You have an azure subscription that contain a virtual named VNet1. VNet1. contains four subnets named Gatesway, perimeter, NVA, and production. The NVA contain two network virtual appliance (NVAs) that will network traffic inspection between the perimeter subnet and the production subnet.

You need to implement an Azure load balancer for the NVAs. The solution must meet the following requirements: The
NVAs must run in an active active configuration that uses automatic failover.
The NVA must load balance traffic to two services on the Production subnet. The services have different IP addresses
Which three actions should you perform? Each correct answer presents parts of the solution.
NOTE: Each correct selection is worth one point.
A. Add two load balancing rules that have HA Ports enabled and Floating IP disabled.
B. Deploy a standard load balancer.
C. Add a frontend IP configuration, two backend pools, and a health prob.
D. Add a frontend IP configuration, a backend pool, and a health probe.
E. Add two load balancing rules that have HA Ports and Floating IP enabled.
F. Deploy a basic load balancer.

Answer: BCE
QUESTION 120
-(4)
You have an Azure subscription named Subscription1.
You have 5 TB of data that you need to transfer to Subscription1. You plan to use an Azure Import/Export job. What can you use as the destination of the imported data?

A. Azure Data Lake Store
B. a virtual machine
C. the Azure File Sync Storage Sync Service
D. Azure Blob storage

Answer: D
QUESTION 121
-(4)
You have an Azure subscription that contains the following resources: 100 Azure virtual machines
20 Azure SQL databases
50 Azure file shares
You need to create a daily backup of all the resources by using Azure Backup. What is the minimum number of backup policies that you must create?

A. 1
B. 2
C. 3
D. 150
E. 170

Answer: C
QUESTION 122
-(4)

You have an Azure subscription that contains a resource group named Test RG. You use TestRG to validate an Azure deployment. TestRG contains the following resources:

Name	Type	Description
VM1	Virtual machine	VM1 is running and configured to backup to valut1 daily.
VAULT1	Recovery services valut	Vault includes all backups of VM1
VNET1	Virtual network	VNET1 has a resource lock of type delete.

You need to delete TestRG.
What should you do first?

A. Modify the backup configurations of VM1 and modify the resource lock type of VNET1.
B. Turn off VM1 and delete all data in Vault1.
C. Remove the resource lock from VNET1 and delete all data in Vault1.
D. Turn off VM1 and remove the resource lock from VNET1.

Answer: D
QUESTION 123
-(4)
You have an Azure subscription that contains a storage account named account1.
You plan to upload the disk files of a virtual machine to account1 from your on premises network. The on premises network uses a public IP address space of 131.107.1.0/24.
You plan to use the disk files to provision an Azure virtual machine named VM1. VM1 will be attached to a virtual network named VNet1. VNet1 uses an IP address space of 192.168.0.0/24.
You need to configure account1 to meet the following requirements: Ensure that you can upload the disk files to account1.
Ensure that you can attach the disks to VM1.
Prevent all other access to account1.
Which two actions should you perform? Each correct selection presents part of the solution.
NOTE: Each correct selection is worth one point.

A. From the Firewalls and virtual networks blade of account1, add the 131.107.1.0/24 IP address range.
B. From the Firewalls and virtual networks blade of account1, select Selected networks.
C. From the Firewalls and virtual networks blade of acount1, add VNet1.
D. From the Firewalls and virtual networks blade of account1, select Allow trusted Microsoft services to access this storage account.
E. From the Service endpoints blade of VNet1, add a service endpoint.

Answer: BE
QUESTION 124
-(4)
You have an Azure virtual machine named VM1.

You use Azure Backup to create a backup of VM1 named Backup1. After creating Backup1, you perform the following changes to VM1: Modify the size of VM1.
Copy a file named Budget.xls to a folder named Data. Reset the password for the built in administrator account.
Add a data disk to VM1.
An administrator uses the Replace existing option to restore VM1 from Backup1. You need to ensure that all the changes to VM1 are restored. Which change should you perform again?

A. Modify the size of VM1.
B. Add a data disk.
C. Reset the password for the built in administrator account.
D. Copy Budget.xls to Data.

Answer: D
QUESTION 125
- (4)
You have an Azure virtual machine named VM1.
The network interface for VM1 is configured as shown in the exhibit. (Click the Exhibit tab.)
You deploy a web server on VM1, and then create a secure website that is accessible by using the HTTPS protocol VM1 is used as a web server only.
You need to ensure that users can connect to the website from the Internet. What should you do?

A. Change the priority of Rule3 to 450.
B. Change the priority of Rule6 to 100
C. DeleteRule1.
D. Create a new inbound rule that allows TCP protocol 443 and configure the protocol to have a priority of 501.

Answer: D
QUESTION 126
- (4)
You have two Azure virtual machines named VM1 and VM2. You have two Recovery Services vaults named RSV1 and RSV2. VM2 is protected by RSV1.
You need to use RSV2 to protect VM2. What should you do first?

A. From the RSV1 blade, click Backup items and stop the VM2 backup.
B. From the RSV1 blade, click Backup Jobs and export the VM2 backup.
C. From the RSV1 blade, click Backu
D. From the Backup blade, select the backup for the virtual machine, and then click Backup.
E. From the VM2 blade, click Disaster recovery, click Replication settings, and then select RSV2 as the Recovery Services vault.

Answer: D
QUESTION 127
- (4)

Note: This question is part of a series of questions that present the same scenario. Each question in the series contains a unique solution that might meet the stated goals. Some question sets might have more than one correct solution, while others might not have a correct solution. After you answer a question in this section, you will NOT be able to return to it. As a result, these questions will not appear in the review screen. You have an Azure subscription that contains the following resources:
A virtual network that has a subnet named Subnet1
Two network security groups (NSGs) named NSG VM1 and NSG Subnet1
A virtual machine named VM1 that has the required Windows Server configurations to allow Remote Desktop connections NSG Subnet1 has the default inbound security rules only.
NSG VM1 has the default inbound security rules and the following custom inbound security rule: Priority: 100
Source: Any
Source port range: * Destination: *
Destination port range: 3389 Protocol: UDP
Action: Allow
VM1 connects to Subnet1. NSG1 VM1 is associated to the network interface of VM1. NSG Subnet1 is associated to Subnet1. You need to be able to establish Remote Desktop connections from the internet to VM1.
Solution: You add an inbound security rule to NSG Subnet1 that allows connections from the Internet source to the Virtual Network destination for port range 3389 and uses the UDP protocol.
Does this meet the goal?

A. Yes
B. No

Answer: B
QUESTION 128
- (4)
You have an Azure Active Directory (Azure AD) tenant named contoso.com. Multi factor authentication (MFA) is enabled for all users. You need to provide users with the ability to bypass MFA for 10 days on devices to which they have successfully signed in by using MFA. What should you do?

A. From the multi factor authentication page, configure the users' settings.
B. From Azure AD, create a conditional access policy.
C. From the multi factor authentication page, configure the service settings.
D. From the MFA blade in Azure AD, configure the MFA Server settings.

Answer: C
QUESTION 129
-
You have an Azure subscription named Subscription1.
You have 5 TB of data that you need to transfer to Subscription1. You plan to use an Azure Import/Export job. What can you use as the destination of the imported data?

E. an Azure Cosmos DB database
F. Azure File Storage
G. the Azure File Sync Storage Sync Service
H. Azure Data Factory

Answer: B
QUESTION 130
- (4)
You have an Azure virtual machine named VM1.
You use Azure Backup to create a backup of VM1 named Backup1. After creating Backup1, you perform the following changes to VM1: Modify the size of VM1.
Copy a file named Budget.xls to a folder named Data. Reset the password for the built in administrator account.
Add a data disk to VM1.
An administrator uses the Replace existing option to restore VM1 from Backup1. You need to ensure that all the changes to VM1 are restored. Which change should you perform again?

E. Modify the size of VM1.
F. Add a data disk.
G. Reset the password for the built in administrator account.
H. Copy Budget.xls to Data.

Answer: D
QUESTION 131
- (4)
You have an Azure subscription that contains a user account named User1.
You need to ensure that User1 can assign a policy to the tenant root management group. What should you do?

E. Assign the Owner role to User1, and then instruct User1 to configure access management for Azure resources.
F. Assign the Global administrator role to User1, and then instruct User1 to configure access management for Azure resources.
G. Assign the Global administrator role to User1, and then modify the default conditional access policies.
H. Assign the Owner role to User1, and then modify the default conditional access policies.

Answer: A
QUESTION 132
- (4)
You download an Azure Resource Manager template based on an existing virtual machine. The template will be used to deploy 100 virtual machines. You need to modify the template to reference an administrative password. You must prevent the password from being stored in plain text.
What should you create to store the password?

E. Azure Active Directory (AD) Identity Protection and an Azure policy
F. a Recovery Services vault and a backup policy
G. an Azure Key Vault and an access policy
H. an Azure Storage account and an access policy

Answer: C
QUESTION 133
- (4)
You create an App Service plan named App1 and an Azure web app named webapp1. You discover that the option to create a staging slot is unavailable. You need to create a staging slot for App1.
What should you do first?

E. From webapp1, modify the Application settings.
F. From webapp1, add a custom domain.
G. From App1, scale up the App Service plan.
H. From App1, scale out the App Service plan.

Answer: C
QUESTION 134
You have an Azure Migrate project that has the following assessment properties: Target location: East US
Storage redundancy: Locally redundant Comfort factor: 2.0
Performance history: 1 month Percentile utilization: 95th Pricing tier: Standard
Offer: Pay as you go
You discover the following two virtual machines:
A virtual machine named VM1 that runs Windows Server 2016 and has 10 CPU cores at 20 percent utilization A virtual machine named VM2 that runs Windows Server 2012 and has four CPU cores at 50 percent utilization
How many CPU cores will Azure Migrate recommend for each virtual machine? To answer, select the appropriate options in the answer area.
NOTE: Each correct selection is worth one point.

VM1:	2
	4
	10
	20
VM2:	1
	2
	4
	8

A. Mastered
B. Not Mastered
Answer: A
QUESTION 135

You have an Azure Active Directory (Azure AD) tenant named contoso.onmicrosoft.com. The User administrator role is assigned to a user named Admin1. An external partner has a Microsoft account that uses the user1@outlook.com sign in.
Admin1 attempts to invite the external partner to sign in to the Azure AD tenant and receives the following error message: "Unable to invite user user1@outlook.com – Generic authorization exception."
You need to ensure that Admin1 can invite the external partner to sign in to the Azure AD tenant.
What should you do?

E. From the Roles and administrators blade, assign the Security administrator role to Admin1.
F. From the Organizational relationships blade, add an identity provider.
G. From the Custom domain names blade, add a custom domain.
H. From the Users blade, modify the External collaboration settings.

Answer: D
QUESTION 136
Note: This question is part of a series of questions that present the same scenario. Each question in the series contains a unique solution that might meet the stated goals. Some question sets might have more than one correct solution, while others might not have a correct solution.
After you answer a question in this section, you will NOT be able to return to it. As a result, these questions will not appear in the review screen. You have an Azure subscription that contains the following resources:
A virtual network that has a subnet named Subnet1
Two network security groups (NSGs) named NSG VM1 and NSG Subnet1
A virtual machine named VM1 that has the required Windows Server configurations to allow Remote Desktop connections NSG Subnet1 has the default inbound security rules only.
NSG VM1 has the default inbound security rules and the following custom inbound security rule: Priority: 100
Source: Any
Source port range: * Destination: *
Destination port range: 3389 Protocol: UDP
Action: Allow
VM1 connects to Subnet1. NSG1 VM1 is associated to the network interface of VM1. NSG Subnet1 is associated to Subnet1. You need to be able to establish Remote Desktop connections from the internet to VM1.
Solution: You add an inbound security rule to NSG Subnet1 and NSG VM1 that allows connections from the internet source to the Virtual Network destination for port range 3389 and uses the TCP protocol.
Does this meet the goal?

C. Yes
D. No

Answer: A
QUESTION 137

Note: This question is part of a series of questions that present the same scenario. Each question in the series contains a unique solution that might meet the stated goals. Some question sets might have more than one correct solution, while others might not have a correct solution. After you answer a question in this section, you will NOT be able to return to it. As a result, these questions will not appear in the review screen.
You have an Azure Active Directory (Azure AD) tenant named Adatum and an Azure Subscription named Subscription1. Adatum contains a group named Developers. Subscription1 contains a resource group named Dev.
You need to provide the Developers group with the ability to create Azure logic apps in the Dev resource group. Solution: On Subscription1, you assign the DevTest Labs User role to the Developers group. Does this meet the goal?

C. Yes
D. No

Answer: B
QUESTION 139
You have an Azure subscription.
Users access the resources in the subscription from either home or from customer sites. From home, users must establish a point to site VPN to access the Azure resources. The users on the customer sites access the Azure resources by using site to site VPNs.
You have a line of business app named App1 that runs on several Azure virtual machine. The virtual machines run Windows Server 2016. You need to ensure that the connections to App1 are spread across all the virtual machines.
What are two possible Azure services that you can use? Each correct answer presents a complete solution. NOTE: Each correct selection is worth one point.

F. a public load balancer
G. Traffic Manager
H. an Azure Content Delivery Network (CDN)
I. an internal load balancer
J. an Azure Application Gateway

Answer: DE
QUESTION 140
Note: This question is part of a series of questions that present the same scenario. Each question in the series contains a unique solution that might meet the stated goals. Some question sets might have more than one correct solution, while others might not have a correct solution. After you answer a question in this section, you will NOT be able to return to it. As a result, these questions will not appear in the review screen.
You have an Azure Active Directory (Azure AD) tenant named Adatum and an Azure Subscription named Subscription1. Adatum contains a group named Developers. Subscription1 contains a resource group named Dev.
You need to provide the Developers group with the ability to create Azure logic apps in the Dev resource group. Solution: On Dev, you assign the Contributor role to the Developers group. Does this meet the goal?

C. Yes
D. No

Answer: A
QUESTION 141
You need to resolve the licensing issue before you attempt to assign the license again. What should you do?

D. From the Groups blade, invite the user accounts to a new group.
E. From the Profile blade, modify the usage location.
F. From the Directory role blade, modify the directory role.

Answer: B
QUESTION 142
You have two subscriptions named Subscription1 and Subscription2. Each subscription is associated to a different Azure AD tenant.
Subscription1 contains a virtual network named VNet1.VNet1 contains an Azure virtual machine named VM1 and has an IP address space of 10.0.0.0/16. Subscription2 contains a virtual network named VNet2. VNet2 contains an Azure virtual machine named VM2 and has an IP address space of 10.10.0.0/24. You need to connect VNet1 to VNet2. What should you do first?

E. Move VNet1 to Subscription2.
F. Modify the IP address space of VNet2.
G. Provision virtual network gateways.
H. Move VM1 to Subscription2.

Answer: C
QUESTION 143
You have an on premises server that contains a folder named D:\Folder1.
You need to copy the contents of D:\Folder1 to the public container in an Azure Storage account named contoso data. Which command should you run?

E. https://contosodata.blob.core.windows.net/public
F. azcopy sync D:\folder1 https://contosodata.blob.core.windows.net/public snapshot
G. azcopy copy D:\folder1 https://contosodata.blob.core.windows.net/public recursive
H. az storage blob copy start batch D:\Folder1 https:// contosodata.blob.core.windows.net/public

Answer: C
QUESTION 144
Your on premises network contains an SMB share named Share1. You have an Azure subscription that contains the following resources: A web app named webapp1
A virtual network named VNET1
You need to ensure that webapp1 can connect to Share1. What should you deploy?

D. an Azure Application Gateway

E. an Azure Active Directory (Azure AD) Application Proxy
F. an Azure Virtual Network Gateway

Answer: F
QUESTION 145
You have an Azure Active Directory (Azure AD) domain that contains 5,000 user accounts. You create a new user account named AdminUser1. You need to assign the User administrator administrative role to AdminUser1. What should you do from the user account properties?
D. From the Directory role blade, modify the directory role.
E. From the Groups blade, invite the user account to a new group.
F. From the Licenses blade, assign a new license.

Answer: D
QUESTION 146

You have an Azure Active Directory (Azure AD) tenant named contoso.onmicrosoft.com that contains 100 user accounts. You purchase 10 Azure AD Premium P2 licenses for the tenant. You need to ensure that 10 users can use all the Azure AD Premium features. What should you do?

E. From the Groups blade of each user, invite the users to a group.
F. From the Licenses blade of Azure AD, assign a license.
G. From the Directory role blade of each user, modify the directory role.
H. From the Azure AD domain, add an enterprise application.

Answer: B

ONLINE RESOURCES

Practice Paper
Link : https://forms.gle/weGfqm94ZfbqFMQ88

QR Code :

Video Content
Link : https://www.youtube.com/playlist?list=PLzlh_31VWEFq7JHJMuPJZcw-XShaPrUYP

QR Code :

Chapter 3: Viva Voce Questions

Q 1: What is Microsoft Azure used for?
Answer: Microsoft Azure is used for building, testing, deploying, and managing applications and services through Microsoft-managed data centers, offering cloud services like computing, analytics, storage, and networking.
Q 2: What are the core responsibilities of an Azure Administrator?
Answer: Azure Administrators manage services related to computing, storage, network, and security. They oversee the Azure environment to ensure it is optimally configured, secured, and maintained.
Q 3: How does Azure Active Directory differ from on-premises AD?
Answer: Azure Active Directory is an identity service providing additional cloud-based features like multi-factor authentication, device registration, and application management, whereas on-premises AD is focused on traditional domain services.
Q 4: Can you explain Azure Resource Manager?
Answer: Azure Resource Manager is a management layer that allows you to create, update, and delete resources in your Azure account. It organizes resources into groups and provides a consistent management layer.
Q 5: What is the role of Azure Policy?
Answer: Azure Policy is a service in Azure that helps you enforce organizational standards and assess compliance at scale through policy definitions that are assigned to resources and resource groups.
Q 6: How do you automate tasks in Azure?
Answer: Tasks in Azure can be automated using Azure Automation, PowerShell scripts, or Azure Logic Apps, allowing for repetitive procedures to be automated for efficiency and accuracy.
Q 7: Describe the Azure Backup service.
Answer: Azure Backup service provides backup for data in the cloud and on-premises environments, helping to protect against data loss and ransomware attacks.
Q 8: What is Azure Virtual Network?
Answer: Azure Virtual Network is the fundamental building block for your private network in Azure. It enables Azure resources to securely communicate with each other, the internet, and on-premises networks.
Q 9: Explain the concept of Azure Load Balancer.
Answer: Azure Load Balancer is a Layer-4 (TCP, UDP) load balancer that provides high availability by distributing incoming traffic among healthy service instances in cloud services or virtual machines.
Q 10: What is Azure Monitor?
Answer: Azure Monitor collects, analyzes, and acts on telemetry data from cloud and on-premises environments, helping to understand how applications are performing and proactively identify issues affecting them.
Q 11: How does Azure ensure data security and compliance?
Answer: Azure secures data through layered security measures including network security, encryption, access control, and threat intelligence, while compliance is ensured through rigorous audits and certifications.
Q 12: What is the use of Azure Service Health?

Answer: Azure Service Health provides personalized alerts and guidance when Azure service issues affect you. It informs about service outages, planned maintenance, and health advisories.

Q 13: Can you migrate on-premises virtual machines to Azure? How?

Answer: Yes, on-premises virtual machines can be migrated to Azure using Azure Migrate, which assesses on-premises environments, provides guidance, and performs the migration.

Q 14: What are network security groups (NSGs) in Azure?

Answer: NSGs are used to filter network traffic to and from Azure resources in an Azure virtual network. An NSG contains security rules that allow or deny inbound or outbound network traffic.

Q 15: What are Azure managed disks?

Answer: Azure managed disks are block-level storage volumes that are managed by Azure and used with Azure Virtual Machines. They are like physical disks in an on-premises server but virtualized.

Q 16: Explain scaling in Azure.

Answer: Scaling in Azure refers to the ability to increase or decrease resources based on demand. Azure provides both vertical scaling (changing the size of an instance) and horizontal scaling (adding more instances).

Q 17: What is Azure ExpressRoute?

Answer: Azure ExpressRoute is a service that provides a private connection between an organization's on-premises infrastructure and Microsoft Azure. This bypasses the internet to offer more reliability, faster speeds, lower latencies, and higher security.

Q 18: How do Azure subscriptions work?

Answer: Azure subscriptions are a logical unit of Azure services that link to an Azure account, which is billed separately; it provides a grouping of resources under a single billing unit.

Q 19: What is Azure Storage Explorer?

Answer: Azure Storage Explorer is a standalone app that enables you to easily work with Azure Storage data on Windows, macOS, and Linux.

Q 20: Describe the role of an Azure Traffic Manager.

Answer: Azure Traffic Manager is a DNS-based traffic load balancer that distributes network traffic optimally to services across global Azure regions, while providing high availability and responsiveness.

YouTube Link for Viva Voce Questions:
https://www.youtube.com/playlist?list=PLzlh_31VWEFq9gJJmCfiH9O2oEqa7SAR

QR Code:

YouTube Videos Playlists for all Microsoft Certifications Videos

Microsoft Azure AI Fundamentals AZ-900
Link: https://www.youtube.com/playlist?list=PLzlh_31VWEFq9KU8Gr0ISbfj-TW6k17f8

QR Code:

Microsoft Azure Administrator AZ-104 Microsoft Azure Virtual Desktop AZ-140
Link: https://www.youtube.com/playlist?list=PLzlh_31VWEFq7JHJMuPJZcw-XShaPrUYP

QR Code:

Microsoft Azure Virtual Desktop AZ-140
Link: https://www.youtube.com/playlist?list=PLzlh_31VWEFowmPK_ro41wiljGoGKexGI

QR Code:

Microsoft Azure Developer AZ-204
Link:
https://www.youtube.com/playlist?list=PLzlh_31VWEFqT72UPVCUi6rqRqLBuwMSr

QR Code:

Designing Microsoft Azure Infrastructure Solution AZ-305
Link:
https://www.youtube.com/playlist?list=PLzlh_31VWEFpTerOknh9kgL4eTbhQwDND

QR Code:

Microsoft Azure Devops Engineer AZ-400
Link: https://www.youtube.com/playlist?list=PLzlh_31VWEFpyUIe_DuaeIkcThEfMT_BT

QR Code:

Microsoft Azure Security Engineer AZ-500
Link:
https://www.youtube.com/playlist?list=PLzlh_31VWEFqFBJgQTPNucIO0wVJdjNmS

QR Code:

Microsoft Azure Network Engineer AZ-700
Link:
https://www.youtube.com/playlist?list=PLzlh_31VWEFowujgDl16YDCvsQtmKgEqL

QR Code:

Microsoft Azure Fundamentals AZ-900
Link: https://www.youtube.com/playlist?list=PLzlh_31VWEFpeXZ2p32R1zDsgcbV8kI1K

QR Code:

Microsoft Azure Data Engineer DP-203
Link: https://www.youtube.com/playlist?list=PLzlh_31VWEFp3XTNqoS60UAOzl8NVG-5z

QR Code:

Microsoft Azure Database Administrator DP- 300
Link: https://www.youtube.com/playlist?list=PLzlh_31VWEFpv-rmc2mbpoIqUOqVW_cIo

QR Code:

AZ-104 Practice Questions with Reasoning

1. You need to give a user permission to restart virtual machines but not delete them. Which role should you assign?
A. Owner
B. Contributor
C. Virtual Machine Contributor
D. Reader

Answer: C. Virtual Machine Contributor
Reasoning: Virtual Machine Contributor allows a user to manage virtual machines, including starting, stopping, and restarting them. It does not automatically grant full control over unrelated Azure resources. Owner and Contributor provide broader permissions than required. Reader cannot perform actions such as restarting VMs. In AZ-104, Microsoft often tests least privilege access, so the best answer is the role that gives only the required permissions.

2. A company wants to apply a naming rule to all newly created resources. What should you use?
A. Azure Policy
B. Azure Monitor
C. Azure Advisor
D. Azure Cost Management

Answer: A. Azure Policy
Reasoning: Azure Policy is used to enforce organizational standards and compliance rules. You can create policies that require specific naming patterns, allowed locations, required tags, or allowed resource types. Azure Monitor is for observability, Azure Advisor gives recommendations, and Cost Management tracks spending. For governance rules, Azure Policy is the correct service.

3. You need to prevent accidental deletion of a resource group. What should you configure?
A. Tag
B. Resource lock
C. Azure Policy initiative
D. Management group

Answer: B. Resource lock
Reasoning: A resource lock can prevent accidental deletion or modification of Azure resources. A Delete lock allows users to read and modify a resource but prevents deletion. A ReadOnly lock prevents both deletion and modification. Tags help organize resources but do not protect them. Azure Policy can enforce rules, but a lock is the direct protection against accidental deletion.

4. Which Azure storage redundancy option provides protection against regional failure?
A. LRS
B. ZRS
C. GRS

D. Premium LRS

Answer: C. GRS
Reasoning: Geo-redundant storage replicates data to a secondary Azure region, protecting against regional outages. Locally redundant storage keeps copies in a single datacenter. Zone-redundant storage replicates across availability zones in one region. Premium LRS is still local redundancy. For protection from full regional failure, GRS or GZRS is required.

5. You need to allow temporary read access to a blob without giving the storage account key. What should you use?
A. Access key
B. SAS token
C. Resource lock
D. Azure Policy

Answer: B. SAS token
Reasoning: A Shared Access Signature provides limited and time-bound access to Azure Storage resources. You can define permissions such as read, write, or delete, and set start and expiry times. Storage account keys provide broad access and should not be shared unless necessary. SAS is the better choice for temporary delegated access.

6. Which tool is commonly used to copy large amounts of data to Azure Blob Storage from the command line?
A. Azure Advisor
B. AzCopy
C. Azure Policy
D. Network Watcher

Answer: B. AzCopy
Reasoning: AzCopy is a command-line utility used to copy blobs or files to and from Azure Storage. It is commonly tested in AZ-104 for data transfer scenarios. Azure Advisor gives optimization recommendations. Azure Policy enforces governance. Network Watcher helps diagnose network issues.

7. You need to make sure only selected virtual networks can access a storage account. What should you configure?
A. Storage firewall and virtual network rules
B. Blob soft delete
C. Lifecycle management
D. Access tier

Answer: A. Storage firewall and virtual network rules
Reasoning: Storage account firewalls and virtual network rules restrict access based on network origin. This is useful when you want only approved VNets, subnets, or IP ranges to access a storage account. Blob soft delete protects deleted data. Lifecycle management moves or deletes data based on rules. Access tiers control storage cost and performance.

8. A VM must remain available during datacenter failure within a region. What should you use?
A. Availability set
B. Availability zone
C. Proximity placement group
D. Scale set only

Answer: B. Availability zone
Reasoning: Availability zones are physically separate datacenters within an Azure region. Deploying VMs across zones protects workloads from datacenter-level failures. Availability sets protect against hardware rack or update domain failures but not full datacenter failure. Proximity placement groups reduce latency but do not provide high availability.

9. You need to deploy identical VMs and automatically increase the number of instances based on demand. What should you use?
A. Availability set
B. Virtual Machine Scale Set
C. Azure Bastion
D. Azure DNS

Answer: B. Virtual Machine Scale Set
Reasoning: Virtual Machine Scale Sets allow you to deploy and manage a group of identical load-balanced VMs. They support autoscaling based on metrics such as CPU usage. Availability sets improve VM availability but do not automatically scale. Azure Bastion provides secure RDP/SSH access. Azure DNS manages domain records.

10. You need secure browser-based RDP access to a VM without exposing port 3389 publicly. What should you use?
A. Public IP
B. Azure Bastion
C. NAT Gateway
D. Application Gateway

Answer: B. Azure Bastion
Reasoning: Azure Bastion provides secure RDP and SSH connectivity through the Azure portal without assigning a public IP to the VM. It helps reduce exposure to internet-based attacks. A public IP with open RDP is less secure. NAT Gateway provides outbound internet connectivity. Application Gateway is for HTTP/HTTPS traffic management.

11. What is the default rule behavior of a Network Security Group?
A. Allow all inbound traffic
B. Deny all outbound traffic
C. Deny inbound traffic from the internet
D. Allow inbound traffic from the internet

Answer: C. Deny inbound traffic from the internet

Reasoning: NSGs contain default security rules. By default, inbound traffic from the internet is denied, while traffic inside a virtual network and from Azure load balancers is allowed. Outbound internet traffic is allowed by default. AZ-104 often tests how NSG rules are evaluated using priority numbers and default rules.

12. You need to connect two Azure virtual networks in the same region. What should you configure?
A. VNet peering
B. VPN Gateway only
C. Azure Firewall only
D. Azure Monitor

Answer: A. VNet peering
Reasoning: VNet peering connects two Azure virtual networks and allows private IP communication between them. It can be used within the same region or across regions using global VNet peering. VPN Gateway can also connect networks, but peering is simpler and provides low-latency private connectivity for Azure VNets.

13. You need outbound internet access for VMs in a private subnet using a fixed public IP. What should you use?
A. NAT Gateway
B. Azure Bastion
C. Private Endpoint
D. Azure DNS private zone

Answer: A. NAT Gateway
Reasoning: NAT Gateway provides scalable outbound internet connectivity for resources in a subnet. It can use one or more static public IP addresses. Azure Bastion is for secure management access. Private Endpoint connects privately to Azure PaaS services. Private DNS zones provide name resolution, not outbound internet access.

14. You need to privately access an Azure Storage account from a VNet without using the public endpoint. What should you configure?
A. Public IP
B. Private Endpoint
C. Load Balancer
D. Traffic Manager

Answer: B. Private Endpoint
Reasoning: A Private Endpoint gives an Azure PaaS service a private IP address from your virtual network. This allows private connectivity to services such as Storage, SQL Database, and Key Vault. It avoids public internet exposure. Load Balancer distributes traffic to compute resources. Traffic Manager performs DNS-based routing.

15. Which service collects metrics and logs from Azure resources?
A. Azure Monitor

B. Azure Policy
C. Azure Blueprints
D. Azure Cost Management

Answer: A. Azure Monitor
Reasoning: Azure Monitor collects, analyzes, and acts on telemetry from Azure and hybrid resources. It includes metrics, logs, alerts, dashboards, and Log Analytics. Azure Policy handles governance. Cost Management tracks spending. Azure Monitor is the primary service for observability and alerting in AZ-104.

16. You need to query log data using KQL. Where should you run the query?
A. Azure Advisor
B. Log Analytics workspace
C. Azure Policy
D. Azure Resource Graph only

Answer: B. Log Analytics workspace
Reasoning: Log Analytics workspaces store log data collected by Azure Monitor. You use Kusto Query Language to query and analyze that data. Azure Resource Graph also uses KQL-like queries, but it is mainly for resource inventory. For monitoring logs, Log Analytics is the expected answer.

17. You need to receive an email when CPU usage on a VM exceeds 90%. What should you create?
A. Alert rule and action group
B. Resource lock
C. Availability set
D. Azure Policy assignment

Answer: A. Alert rule and action group
Reasoning: Azure Monitor alert rules define the condition, such as CPU greater than 90%. Action groups define what happens when the alert fires, such as sending email, SMS, webhook, or automation action. Resource locks protect resources. Availability sets provide VM availability. Policy enforces compliance.

18. Which Azure service provides backup for Azure virtual machines?
A. Recovery Services vault
B. Azure Firewall
C. Azure Bastion
D. Azure Load Balancer

Answer: A. Recovery Services vault
Reasoning: Recovery Services vault stores backup data and recovery points for Azure VMs and other workloads. You configure backup policies, retention, and restore operations through the vault. Azure Firewall secures network traffic. Bastion provides secure VM access. Load Balancer distributes traffic but does not provide backup.

19. A user needs to manage all resources in a subscription, including assigning access to others. Which role is required?
A. Reader
B. Contributor
C. Owner
D. Storage Blob Data Reader

Answer: C. Owner
Reasoning: Owner has full management access to Azure resources and can assign roles to other users. Contributor can manage resources but cannot grant access. Reader can only view resources. Storage Blob Data Reader is limited to reading blob data. Role assignment permission is the key difference between Owner and Contributor.

20. You want to organize multiple subscriptions and apply governance at scale. What should you use?
A. Resource group
B. Management group
C. Availability set
D. Storage account

Answer: B. Management group
Reasoning: Management groups provide a hierarchy above subscriptions. They are used to apply Azure Policy, RBAC, and governance controls across multiple subscriptions. Resource groups organize resources inside a subscription. Availability sets relate to VM availability. Storage accounts store data.

21. Which feature helps recover accidentally deleted blobs?
A. Blob soft delete
B. Azure Bastion
C. NAT Gateway
D. Azure Advisor

Answer: A. Blob soft delete
Reasoning: Blob soft delete protects blobs from accidental deletion by retaining deleted data for a configured retention period. During that period, the blob can be restored. This is different from redundancy, which protects against infrastructure failure. Soft delete protects against user or application deletion mistakes.

22. You need to automatically move old blob data to a cool tier. What should you configure?
A. Lifecycle management rule
B. Resource lock
C. Azure Policy exemption
D. Availability zone

Answer: A. Lifecycle management rule

Reasoning: Blob lifecycle management lets you automatically move data between access tiers or delete data based on conditions such as age or last modified date. This helps reduce storage costs. Resource locks prevent deletion or modification. Azure Policy can enforce configuration but does not move blobs by age.

23. Which storage access tier is best for frequently accessed data?
A. Archive
B. Cool
C. Hot
D. Offline

Answer: C. Hot
Reasoning: The Hot tier is optimized for frequently accessed data. Cool is for infrequently accessed data stored for at least 30 days. Archive is for rarely accessed data with retrieval latency. There is no standard Azure Blob access tier called Offline. AZ-104 often tests choosing the correct tier based on access pattern and cost.

24. You need to create a repeatable deployment of Azure resources using JSON or Bicep. What should you use?
A. ARM template
B. Azure Advisor
C. Azure Monitor alert
D. Recovery Services vault

Answer: A. ARM template
Reasoning: ARM templates and Bicep are infrastructure-as-code options for Azure deployments. They allow repeatable, declarative resource deployment. Azure Advisor provides recommendations. Azure Monitor alerts detect conditions. Recovery Services vault handles backup and recovery.

25. Which Azure service distributes HTTP and HTTPS traffic at Layer 7?
A. Azure Load Balancer
B. Application Gateway
C. NAT Gateway
D. Network Security Group

Answer: B. Application Gateway
Reasoning: Azure Application Gateway is a Layer 7 load balancer for web traffic. It supports HTTP/HTTPS routing, SSL termination, URL-based routing, and Web Application Firewall. Azure Load Balancer works at Layer 4. NAT Gateway handles outbound connectivity. NSGs filter network traffic.

26. Which Azure service distributes TCP and UDP traffic at Layer 4?
A. Azure Load Balancer
B. Application Gateway
C. Azure DNS

D. Azure Policy

Answer: A. Azure Load Balancer
Reasoning: Azure Load Balancer operates at Layer 4 and distributes TCP and UDP traffic across backend resources. Application Gateway operates at Layer 7 for HTTP and HTTPS. Azure DNS manages DNS records. Azure Policy enforces governance rules. Understanding Layer 4 versus Layer 7 load balancing is important for AZ-104.

27. You need name resolution for private resources inside a virtual network. What should you use?
A. Azure Private DNS zone
B. Public DNS zone only
C. Azure Advisor
D. Azure Policy

Answer: A. Azure Private DNS zone
Reasoning: Azure Private DNS zones provide DNS name resolution within and across virtual networks. They are commonly used with private endpoints so services resolve to private IP addresses. Public DNS zones are for internet-facing name resolution. Advisor and Policy do not provide DNS resolution.

28. A VM has no public IP. You need to connect using SSH securely from the Azure portal. What should you use?
A. Azure Bastion
B. Public Load Balancer
C. NAT Gateway
D. Application Security Group

Answer: A. Azure Bastion
Reasoning: Azure Bastion allows secure RDP and SSH access to VMs through the Azure portal without exposing public IPs. This improves security by avoiding open management ports on the internet. NAT Gateway is for outbound traffic. Load Balancer distributes incoming traffic. Application Security Groups simplify NSG rule targeting.

29. You need to group servers logically for NSG rules without using IP addresses. What should you use?
A. Application Security Groups
B. Availability zones
C. Azure Policy
D. Recovery Services vault

Answer: A. Application Security Groups
Reasoning: Application Security Groups allow you to group virtual machines logically and reference those groups in NSG rules. This avoids maintaining IP-based rules. Availability zones improve resiliency. Azure Policy enforces governance. Recovery Services vault provides backup and recovery.

30. You need to check Azure recommendations for cost, security, reliability, and performance. What should you use?
A. Azure Advisor
B. Azure Bastion
C. Azure DNS
D. Azure Load Balancer

Answer: A. Azure Advisor
Reasoning: Azure Advisor analyzes deployed resources and provides recommendations across cost, security, reliability, operational excellence, and performance. It helps administrators improve Azure environments. Azure Bastion, DNS, and Load Balancer are specific infrastructure services, not recommendation engines.

31. You need to assign access to a user for a single resource only. What scope should you use?

A. Management group
B. Subscription
C. Resource group
D. Resource

Answer: D. Resource
Reasoning: Azure RBAC allows assigning roles at different scopes: management group, subscription, resource group, or individual resource. To follow the principle of least privilege, access should be granted at the smallest scope possible. If the user only needs access to one resource, assigning the role directly at the resource level avoids unnecessary permissions elsewhere. Higher scopes would grant broader access, which is not recommended for security.

32. Which feature ensures that only compliant resources are deployed?

A. Azure Monitor
B. Azure Policy
C. Azure Advisor
D. Azure Backup

Answer: B. Azure Policy
Reasoning: Azure Policy evaluates resources for compliance and can enforce rules during deployment. Policies can deny non-compliant resources or audit them. This helps organizations maintain standards such as allowed regions, required tags, or specific configurations. Azure Monitor observes performance, Advisor suggests improvements, and Backup protects data. Policy is the enforcement tool.

33. You want to track changes made to resources over time. What should you use?

A. Activity Log
B. Azure DNS
C. NSG flow logs
D. Azure Bastion

Answer: A. Activity Log
Reasoning: The Azure Activity Log records all control-plane actions such as resource creation, deletion, and modification. It helps track administrative changes and identify who performed them. NSG flow logs track network traffic, not configuration changes. Azure DNS resolves names, and Bastion enables secure access. For auditing changes, Activity Log is correct.

34. Which storage type supports hierarchical namespace for big data analytics?

A. Blob Storage standard
B. Azure Data Lake Storage Gen2
C. File Storage

D. Queue Storage

Answer: B. Azure Data Lake Storage Gen2
Reasoning: Azure Data Lake Storage Gen2 builds on Blob Storage and adds a hierarchical namespace, making it suitable for big data analytics workloads. It supports directory structures and high-performance analytics. Standard Blob Storage lacks advanced hierarchical features. File Storage is for SMB/NFS shares, and Queue Storage handles messages.

35. You need to mount a storage service as a network drive in Windows. What should you use?

A. Blob Storage
B. File Storage
C. Queue Storage
D. Table Storage

Answer: B. File Storage
Reasoning: Azure File Storage provides SMB (and NFS) shares that can be mounted as a network drive on Windows, Linux, or macOS systems. Blob Storage is for object storage accessed via REST APIs. Queue Storage is for messaging. Table Storage is for NoSQL structured data. For file shares, File Storage is the correct choice.

36. What is the purpose of a subnet in Azure?

A. Store data
B. Segment a virtual network
C. Provide DNS
D. Monitor traffic

Answer: B. Segment a virtual network
Reasoning: A subnet divides a virtual network into smaller logical sections. This allows better organization, security, and routing control. Subnets can be associated with NSGs and route tables. They help isolate workloads such as web, application, and database tiers. Storage and DNS are handled by separate services.

37. Which service helps troubleshoot network connectivity issues?

A. Azure Advisor
B. Network Watcher
C. Azure Bastion
D. Azure Backup

Answer: B. Network Watcher
Reasoning: Network Watcher provides tools like IP flow verify, connection troubleshoot, packet capture, and NSG flow logs. These help diagnose connectivity issues in Azure networks. Azure Advisor gives recommendations. Bastion enables secure access. Backup handles data protection. Network troubleshooting is handled by Network Watcher.

38. You want to filter inbound traffic to a VM. What should you use?

A. NSG
B. Route table
C. Azure Policy
D. Azure Monitor

Answer: A. NSG
Reasoning: Network Security Groups control inbound and outbound traffic to Azure resources using security rules. Rules can allow or deny traffic based on IP, port, and protocol. Route tables control routing paths, not filtering. Azure Policy enforces governance rules. Monitor collects metrics and logs.

39. You need to route traffic through a virtual appliance. What should you configure?

A. NSG
B. Route table (UDR)
C. Azure DNS
D. Availability set

Answer: B. Route table (UDR)
Reasoning: User Defined Routes (UDR) allow custom routing of traffic within Azure networks. You can direct traffic to a virtual appliance such as a firewall or NVA. NSGs filter traffic but do not control routing paths. DNS resolves names, and availability sets provide resiliency.

40. What is the main purpose of Azure DNS?

A. Store data
B. Resolve domain names
C. Monitor applications
D. Secure networks

Answer: B. Resolve domain names
Reasoning: Azure DNS hosts DNS domains and resolves domain names to IP addresses. It supports public and private DNS zones. This service ensures reliable name resolution for applications. It does not store application data, monitor systems, or enforce security policies.

41. You need to scale VMs automatically based on CPU usage. What should you use?

A. Availability set
B. VM Scale Set autoscaling
C. Azure Policy
D. Azure Backup

Answer: B. VM Scale Set autoscaling

Reasoning: VM Scale Sets support autoscaling based on metrics like CPU, memory, or custom metrics. This ensures performance during high demand and reduces cost during low usage. Availability sets improve availability but do not scale. Policy enforces rules. Backup protects data.

42. Which feature ensures VM disk data is encrypted at rest?

A. Azure Firewall
B. Azure Disk Encryption
C. Azure Monitor
D. Azure Advisor

Answer: B. Azure Disk Encryption
Reasoning: Azure Disk Encryption uses BitLocker (Windows) or DM-Crypt (Linux) to encrypt OS and data disks. It protects data at rest. Azure Firewall secures networks, Monitor tracks metrics, and Advisor provides recommendations.

43. Which Azure service helps store secrets like passwords securely?

A. Azure Key Vault
B. Azure Storage
C. Azure Monitor
D. Azure DNS

Answer: A. Azure Key Vault
Reasoning: Azure Key Vault securely stores secrets, keys, and certificates. It provides controlled access and auditing. It is commonly used by applications to retrieve sensitive information securely. Storage stores data, Monitor tracks logs, DNS resolves names.

44. You need to assign policies to multiple subscriptions. What should you use?

A. Resource group
B. Management group
C. Virtual network
D. Storage account

Answer: B. Management group
Reasoning: Management groups allow centralized governance across multiple subscriptions. Policies and RBAC roles can be applied at this level and inherited by all subscriptions. Resource groups apply only within one subscription.

45. Which Azure service provides centralized logging and analytics?

A. Azure Monitor
B. Azure Advisor
C. Azure Policy

D. Azure Bastion

Answer: A. Azure Monitor
Reasoning: Azure Monitor collects metrics and logs from resources and provides insights through Log Analytics. It supports dashboards, alerts, and queries. Advisor gives recommendations. Policy enforces compliance. Bastion provides secure access.

46. You want to ensure all resources have a tag named "Department". What should you use?

A. Azure Monitor
B. Azure Policy
C. NSG
D. Azure DNS

Answer: B. Azure Policy
Reasoning: Azure Policy can enforce tagging rules. You can create policies that require specific tags or even automatically add them. Tags help with cost management and organization. Monitor tracks data but does not enforce tags.

47. Which service provides DDoS protection for Azure resources?

A. Azure Firewall
B. Azure DDoS Protection
C. Azure Monitor
D. Azure Advisor

Answer: B. Azure DDoS Protection
Reasoning: Azure DDoS Protection protects applications from distributed denial-of-service attacks. It provides automatic attack mitigation. Firewall filters traffic, Monitor tracks metrics, Advisor provides recommendations.

48. You need to distribute traffic globally based on user location. What should you use?

A. Azure Load Balancer
B. Traffic Manager
C. NSG
D. NAT Gateway

Answer: B. Traffic Manager
Reasoning: Azure Traffic Manager uses DNS-based routing to direct users to the closest or healthiest endpoint globally. Load Balancer works within a region. NSG filters traffic. NAT Gateway handles outbound traffic.

49. Which storage service is best for unstructured data like images?

A. Blob Storage

B. Table Storage
C. Queue Storage
D. File Storage

Answer: A. Blob Storage
Reasoning: Blob Storage is optimized for storing large amounts of unstructured data such as images, videos, and backups. Table Storage is for structured NoSQL data. Queue Storage handles messages. File Storage is for file shares.

50. Which Azure feature allows rollback of deployments?

A. Azure Monitor
B. ARM template deployment history
C. Azure Policy
D. Azure DNS

Answer: B. ARM template deployment history
Reasoning: ARM tracks deployment history, allowing administrators to review and redeploy previous configurations. This helps rollback changes if needed. Monitor observes metrics. Policy enforces compliance. DNS resolves names.

51. What is the primary purpose of Azure Firewall?

A. Store data
B. Filter network traffic centrally
C. Monitor logs
D. Manage identities

Answer: B. Filter network traffic centrally
Reasoning: Azure Firewall is a managed, cloud-based network security service that protects Azure Virtual Network resources. It allows you to create, enforce, and log application and network connectivity policies across subscriptions and VNets. Unlike NSGs, which are distributed, Azure Firewall provides centralized control. It supports features like threat intelligence filtering, application rules, and NAT rules. It is commonly used in hub-and-spoke network architectures.

52. What is a Public IP address used for in Azure?

A. Internal communication
B. Internet-facing access
C. Data storage
D. Encryption

Answer: B. Internet-facing access
Reasoning: A Public IP address allows Azure resources such as virtual machines, load balancers, or application gateways to communicate with the internet. It enables inbound and outbound connectivity from external networks. Without a public IP, resources remain private within the virtual network. Security best practices recommend minimizing public IP usage and using services like Azure Bastion or Application Gateway instead.

53. What is the purpose of an SLA in Azure?

A. Monitor logs
B. Define uptime guarantees
C. Store data
D. Assign roles

Answer: B. Define uptime guarantees
Reasoning: A Service Level Agreement (SLA) defines the expected availability and performance of Azure services. For example, Azure VMs deployed in an availability set or zone have higher SLA percentages. SLAs are important for planning high availability and understanding downtime risks. They also determine service credits if uptime commitments are not met.

54. What is Azure Resource Graph used for?

A. Backup
B. Query resources at scale

C. DNS resolution
D. Storage

Answer: B. Query resources at scale
Reasoning: Azure Resource Graph allows administrators to query and explore Azure resources across subscriptions using a KQL-based query language. It is optimized for performance and helps in governance, auditing, and inventory management. Unlike Log Analytics, it focuses on resource metadata rather than logs.

55. What is RBAC in Azure?

A. Backup system
B. Role-Based Access Control
C. Resource monitoring
D. Network routing

Answer: B. Role-Based Access Control
Reasoning: RBAC allows administrators to assign permissions to users, groups, or service principals based on roles. It ensures users only have access to what they need. Roles like Owner, Contributor, and Reader define access levels. RBAC is essential for security and governance in Azure.

56. What is autoscaling in Azure?

A. Manual scaling
B. Automatic adjustment of resources
C. Backup process
D. Monitoring logs

Answer: B. Automatic adjustment of resources
Reasoning: Autoscaling automatically increases or decreases the number of resources based on demand or predefined conditions such as CPU usage or request count. It helps maintain performance and reduce costs. It is commonly used with Virtual Machine Scale Sets and App Services.

57. What is Azure Backup used for?

A. Network security
B. Data protection
C. DNS resolution
D. Role assignment

Answer: B. Data protection
Reasoning: Azure Backup provides centralized backup and recovery for Azure resources such as VMs, databases, and file shares. It ensures business continuity by allowing restoration in case of accidental deletion, corruption, or disasters. It integrates with Recovery Services vault.

58. What is a VPN Gateway used for?

A. Storage
B. Hybrid connectivity
C. Monitoring
D. DNS

Answer: B. Hybrid connectivity
Reasoning: VPN Gateway connects on-premises networks to Azure using encrypted tunnels over the internet. It supports site-to-site and point-to-site connections. It is a key component in hybrid cloud architecture.

59. What is ExpressRoute?

A. Public internet connection
B. Dedicated private connection
C. DNS service
D. Backup service

Answer: B. Dedicated private connection
Reasoning: ExpressRoute provides a private, dedicated connection between on-premises infrastructure and Azure. It does not go over the public internet, offering higher reliability, security, and performance. It is used by enterprises for mission-critical workloads.

60. What is tagging in Azure?

A. Encryption method
B. Metadata for resources
C. Network rule
D. Backup type

Answer: B. Metadata for resources
Reasoning: Tags are key-value pairs assigned to Azure resources. They help organize resources, track costs, and enforce governance. For example, tags like Department, Environment, or Project help in cost allocation and reporting.

61–80 (Advanced Scenario-Based)
61. A company wants to restrict resource creation to only specific regions. What should be used?

A. NSG
B. Azure Policy
C. Azure Monitor
D. Load Balancer

Answer: B. Azure Policy

Reasoning: Azure Policy can restrict resource deployment to specific regions. This ensures compliance with data residency and organizational standards.

62. You need to ensure secure communication between VNets across regions. What should you use?

A. VNet Peering (Global)
B. NSG
C. Azure DNS
D. Azure Monitor

Answer: A. VNet Peering (Global)
Reasoning: Global VNet Peering allows secure, low-latency connectivity between VNets in different regions without using the internet.

63. A VM is not reachable. What tool helps diagnose connectivity?

A. Network Watcher
B. Azure Advisor
C. Azure Policy
D. Azure Backup

Answer: A. Network Watcher
Reasoning: Network Watcher provides troubleshooting tools like connection troubleshoot and IP flow verify.

64. You need to encrypt secrets used by applications. What service is best?

A. Azure Key Vault
B. Azure Storage
C. Azure DNS
D. Azure Monitor

Answer: A. Azure Key Vault
Reasoning: Key Vault securely stores secrets, certificates, and encryption keys with controlled access.

65. Which service provides web application firewall capability?

A. Application Gateway
B. Azure DNS
C. NAT Gateway
D. Azure Backup

Answer: A. Application Gateway

Reasoning: Application Gateway includes Web Application Firewall (WAF) to protect web apps from attacks.

66. You need centralized logging across resources. What should you use?

A. Azure Monitor
B. Azure Policy
C. NSG
D. DNS

Answer: A. Azure Monitor
Reasoning: Azure Monitor aggregates logs and metrics across resources for centralized visibility.

67. Which Azure service helps reduce cost by providing recommendations?

A. Azure Advisor
B. Azure Monitor
C. Azure Policy
D. Azure Firewall

Answer: A. Azure Advisor
Reasoning: Advisor suggests optimizations for cost, performance, and security.

68. You need to protect data from accidental deletion in storage. What should be used?

A. Soft delete
B. NSG
C. Azure Monitor
D. Azure DNS

Answer: A. Soft delete
Reasoning: Soft delete allows recovery of deleted data within a retention period.

69. Which service distributes traffic within a region?

A. Load Balancer
B. Traffic Manager
C. DNS
D. Azure Policy

Answer: A. Load Balancer
Reasoning: Load Balancer distributes traffic across VMs within a region.

70. Which service distributes traffic globally?

A. Traffic Manager

B. NSG
C. Azure Monitor
D. Azure Backup

Answer: A. Traffic Manager
Reasoning: Traffic Manager uses DNS to route users globally.

71. What is the purpose of an Availability Set in Azure?

A. Store data
B. Improve VM availability within a datacenter
C. Provide DNS
D. Monitor logs

Answer: B. Improve VM availability within a datacenter
Reasoning: An Availability Set ensures that virtual machines are distributed across fault domains and update domains. Fault domains protect against hardware failures like rack or power issues, while update domains protect against planned maintenance. This increases uptime and meets SLA requirements. However, it does not protect against full datacenter failures—that requires Availability Zones. AZ-104 often tests the distinction between sets and zones.

72. What is the purpose of an Availability Zone?

A. Backup data
B. Protect against datacenter failure
C. Provide internet access
D. Manage DNS

Answer: B. Protect against datacenter failure
Reasoning: Availability Zones are physically separate datacenters within a region. Deploying resources across zones ensures resilience against complete datacenter outages. Each zone has independent power, cooling, and networking. This provides higher SLA than Availability Sets. AZ-104 exams frequently test when to use zones versus sets for high availability.

73. What is the main purpose of Azure Bastion?

A. Backup data
B. Secure RDP/SSH access via browser
C. DNS resolution
D. Load balancing

Answer: B. Secure RDP/SSH access via browser
Reasoning: Azure Bastion allows secure remote access to virtual machines without exposing public IP addresses. It operates through the Azure portal using HTTPS. This reduces attack surface and improves security posture. It eliminates the need to open ports like 22 or 3389 to the internet.

74. What is the purpose of a NAT Gateway?

A. Inbound traffic filtering
B. Outbound internet access with static IP
C. DNS resolution
D. Monitoring

Answer: B. Outbound internet access with static IP
Reasoning: NAT Gateway provides outbound internet connectivity for resources in a subnet using a static public IP. It ensures predictable outbound IP and scales automatically. It does not accept inbound connections, making it more secure than assigning public IPs to VMs.

75. What is the purpose of a Private Endpoint?

A. Public internet access
B. Secure private access to Azure services
C. Backup data
D. DNS management

Answer: B. Secure private access to Azure services
Reasoning: Private Endpoint assigns a private IP to a PaaS service within your VNet. This ensures traffic stays within the Azure network instead of going over the public internet. It is commonly used for services like Storage, SQL, and Key Vault.

76. What is the purpose of a Route Table (UDR)?

A. Encrypt data
B. Control traffic routing
C. Monitor logs
D. Assign roles

Answer: B. Control traffic routing
Reasoning: User Defined Routes allow administrators to override Azure's default routing behavior. Traffic can be directed through virtual appliances, firewalls, or gateways. This is critical for advanced network designs such as hub-and-spoke.

77. What is the purpose of a Network Security Group (NSG)?

A. Store data
B. Filter network traffic
C. DNS resolution
D. Backup

Answer: B. Filter network traffic
Reasoning: NSGs act as a firewall at subnet or NIC level. They allow or deny inbound/outbound traffic based on rules. Each rule includes priority, source, destination, port, and protocol. NSGs are fundamental for securing Azure networks.

78. What is the purpose of Log Analytics?

A. Backup
B. Query and analyze logs

C. DNS
D. Storage

Answer: B. Query and analyze logs
Reasoning: Log Analytics is part of Azure Monitor and stores log data. It allows querying using KQL for troubleshooting and insights. It supports dashboards, alerts, and automation. It is widely used in AZ-104 scenarios for monitoring.

79. What is the purpose of an Action Group?

A. Store logs
B. Trigger alert actions
C. Manage roles
D. Route traffic

Answer: B. Trigger alert actions
Reasoning: Action Groups define what happens when an alert fires. Actions can include email, SMS, webhook, or automation runbooks. They are linked to alert rules in Azure Monitor. This helps automate responses to issues.

80. What is the purpose of a Recovery Services Vault?

A. DNS
B. Store backup data
C. Route traffic
D. Filter traffic

Answer: B. Store backup data
Reasoning: Recovery Services Vault is used to store backup data and recovery points. It supports VM backups, Azure Files, and on-premises workloads. It ensures secure, centralized backup management.

81–100 (Exam-Level Scenarios)
81. A company wants to ensure only approved VM sizes are used. What should they implement?

A. NSG
B. Azure Policy
C. Azure Monitor
D. Load Balancer

Answer: B. Azure Policy
Reasoning: Azure Policy can restrict VM sizes by defining allowed SKUs. This ensures compliance with cost and performance standards. It can deny non-compliant deployments.

82. You need to monitor application performance across multiple resources. What should you use?

A. Azure Monitor
B. Azure DNS
C. Azure Policy
D. NSG

Answer: A. Azure Monitor
Reasoning: Azure Monitor provides performance metrics, logs, and insights across resources. It helps detect issues and optimize performance.

83. You need to assign permissions to an application. What identity should you use?

A. User account
B. Service Principal
C. Resource group
D. NSG

Answer: B. Service Principal
Reasoning: A Service Principal represents an application identity in Azure. It is used for automation and secure access without using user credentials.

84. A VM must automatically recover from failure. What should you configure?

A. Availability Set
B. NSG
C. Azure Policy
D. DNS

Answer: A. Availability Set
Reasoning: Availability Sets ensure VMs are spread across fault domains, improving resilience and automatic recovery.

85. You need to connect on-premises to Azure securely over the internet. What should you use?

A. VPN Gateway
B. ExpressRoute
C. Load Balancer
D. DNS

Answer: A. VPN Gateway
Reasoning: VPN Gateway provides encrypted communication over the internet. ExpressRoute is private but not over internet.

86. You need high-performance private connectivity. What should you use?

A. VPN Gateway

B. ExpressRoute
C. NSG
D. Azure Monitor

Answer: B. ExpressRoute
Reasoning: ExpressRoute provides dedicated, private, high-speed connectivity without using the public internet.

87. Which service protects against web attacks like SQL injection?

A. NSG
B. WAF
C. NAT Gateway
D. Azure Monitor

Answer: B. WAF
Reasoning: Web Application Firewall protects against OWASP threats like SQL injection and XSS.

88. You need to manage secrets centrally. What should you use?

A. Azure Key Vault
B. Azure Storage
C. NSG
D. Azure DNS

Answer: A. Azure Key Vault
Reasoning: Key Vault securely stores and manages secrets, keys, and certificates.

89. You want to analyze logs using queries. What language is used?

A. SQL
B. KQL
C. Python
D. JSON

Answer: B. KQL
Reasoning: Kusto Query Language (KQL) is used in Azure Monitor and Log Analytics.

90. Which feature helps recover deleted VMs?

A. Backup
B. NSG
C. DNS
D. Policy

Answer: A. Backup
Reasoning: Azure Backup allows restoration of deleted or corrupted VMs.

91. A company needs to distribute user traffic to the nearest region globally. What should be used?

A. Azure Load Balancer
B. Traffic Manager
C. NSG
D. NAT Gateway

Answer: B. Traffic Manager
Reasoning: Azure Traffic Manager is a DNS-based traffic routing service that directs user requests to the closest or most appropriate endpoint based on routing methods such as geographic, priority, or performance. It is ideal for global load distribution across regions. Azure Load Balancer works only within a region, while NSGs and NAT Gateway do not perform traffic distribution.

92. You need to block specific inbound ports to a VM. What should you configure?

A. Azure Policy
B. NSG
C. Azure Monitor
D. Route table

Answer: B. NSG
Reasoning: Network Security Groups allow you to define inbound and outbound rules based on ports, protocols, and IP ranges. To block specific ports like 22 or 3389, you create a deny rule with a higher priority than the default allow rules. Azure Policy enforces compliance but does not filter traffic directly.

93. You want centralized monitoring of logs and metrics. Which service is best?

A. Azure Monitor
B. Azure DNS
C. Azure Policy
D. Azure Advisor

Answer: A. Azure Monitor
Reasoning: Azure Monitor collects, aggregates, and analyzes telemetry data from multiple resources. It includes metrics, logs, alerts, and dashboards. It integrates with Log Analytics for deep insights. DNS resolves names, Policy enforces compliance, and Advisor provides recommendations.

94. You need to logically group related Azure resources. What should you use?

A. Subscription
B. Resource Group
C. Management Group

D. NSG

Answer: B. Resource Group
Reasoning: Resource Groups are containers that hold related resources for an Azure solution. They help manage lifecycle, permissions, and billing. Management groups organize subscriptions, not individual resources. NSGs handle security rules.

95. You need to ensure application availability during datacenter failure. What should you use?

A. Availability Set
B. Availability Zone
C. NSG
D. Azure Monitor

Answer: B. Availability Zone
Reasoning: Availability Zones distribute resources across physically separate datacenters. This ensures resilience even if one datacenter fails. Availability Sets protect only within a single datacenter.

96. You need secure access to a storage account without public internet exposure. What should you use?

A. Public IP
B. Private Endpoint
C. Load Balancer
D. DNS

Answer: B. Private Endpoint
Reasoning: Private Endpoint assigns a private IP to the storage account within a VNet, ensuring traffic stays within Azure's network. This improves security and eliminates exposure to the public internet.

97. You need to control how traffic flows within a VNet. What should you use?

A. NSG
B. Route Table
C. Azure Monitor
D. Azure Backup

Answer: B. Route Table
Reasoning: Route Tables (UDR) define how packets are routed within a network. They allow redirection to virtual appliances or gateways. NSGs filter traffic, but do not control routing paths.

98. You need to encrypt VM disks. What should you use?

A. Azure Disk Encryption

B. Azure Monitor
C. Azure DNS
D. Azure Policy

Answer: A. Azure Disk Encryption
Reasoning: Azure Disk Encryption protects data at rest using BitLocker (Windows) or DM-Crypt (Linux). It integrates with Azure Key Vault for key management.

99. Which service manages user authentication in Azure?

A. Azure AD
B. Azure Monitor
C. Azure DNS
D. Azure Backup

Answer: A. Azure AD
Reasoning: Azure Active Directory (now part of Microsoft Entra ID) handles authentication and identity management. It supports users, groups, and applications.

100. You need to deploy resources repeatedly using code. What should you use?

A. ARM template
B. Azure Monitor
C. Azure DNS
D. Azure Backup

Answer: A. ARM template
Reasoning: ARM templates (or Bicep) allow Infrastructure as Code deployments. They ensure consistency, repeatability, and automation.

101–120 (Advanced Case-Based Questions)
101. A company wants to enforce tagging across all resources automatically. What should they use?

A. Azure Monitor
B. Azure Policy
C. NSG
D. Azure DNS

Answer: B. Azure Policy
Reasoning: Azure Policy can enforce required tags and even auto-apply them. This ensures compliance and helps with cost tracking and governance.

102. You need to provide temporary access to storage resources. What should you use?

A. Access keys

B. SAS token
C. Azure Policy
D. NSG

Answer: B. SAS token
Reasoning: SAS tokens provide limited, time-bound access to storage resources without exposing account keys.

103. You want to analyze log data using queries. What should you use?

A. Azure Monitor Logs
B. Azure DNS
C. Azure Backup
D. Azure Policy

Answer: A. Azure Monitor Logs
Reasoning: Azure Monitor Logs (Log Analytics) allows querying logs using KQL for troubleshooting and analysis.

104. You need to protect against accidental resource deletion. What should you use?

A. Tag
B. Resource Lock
C. NSG
D. Azure Monitor

Answer: B. Resource Lock
Reasoning: Resource locks prevent accidental deletion or modification of resources.

105. You need to allow only HTTPS traffic to a web app. What should you use?

A. NSG
B. Application Gateway
C. Azure DNS
D. Azure Monitor

Answer: B. Application Gateway
Reasoning: Application Gateway supports Layer 7 routing and can enforce HTTPS-only access with SSL termination.

106. You need to connect multiple VNets securely. What should you use?

A. VNet Peering
B. NSG
C. Azure DNS
D. Azure Monitor

Answer: A. VNet Peering
Reasoning: VNet Peering allows secure communication between VNets using private IPs.

107. You want to monitor network traffic flow. What should you use?

A. NSG Flow Logs
B. Azure Policy
C. Azure Backup
D. DNS

Answer: A. NSG Flow Logs
Reasoning: NSG Flow Logs capture traffic data for analysis and troubleshooting.

108. You need to ensure high availability for VMs across regions. What should you use?

A. Availability Set
B. Traffic Manager
C. NSG
D. Azure Monitor

Answer: B. Traffic Manager
Reasoning: Traffic Manager distributes traffic across regions, ensuring failover.

109. You need to control outbound internet traffic. What should you use?

A. NAT Gateway
B. NSG
C. Azure DNS
D. Azure Backup

Answer: A. NAT Gateway
Reasoning: NAT Gateway provides controlled outbound internet connectivity with static IP.

110. You want to secure web applications from attacks. What should you use?

A. WAF
B. NSG
C. Azure Monitor
D. DNS

Answer: A. WAF
Reasoning: Web Application Firewall protects against common web vulnerabilities.

111. You need to monitor performance metrics like CPU and memory across Azure resources. What should you use?

A. Azure Monitor
B. Azure Policy
C. Azure DNS
D. Azure Backup

Answer: A. Azure Monitor
Reasoning: Azure Monitor is the primary service for collecting and analyzing metrics such as CPU usage, memory utilization, and disk I/O. It provides real-time insights, dashboards, and alerting capabilities. Metrics are lightweight numerical data collected at regular intervals. Azure Policy enforces rules, DNS resolves names, and Backup handles recovery. For performance monitoring and proactive alerting, Azure Monitor is the correct choice.

112. You need to securely store application secrets like API keys and passwords. Which service should you use?

A. Azure Storage
B. Azure Key Vault
C. Azure Monitor
D. Azure DNS

Answer: B. Azure Key Vault
Reasoning: Azure Key Vault is designed to securely store and manage sensitive information such as secrets, encryption keys, and certificates. It provides role-based access control, auditing, and integration with Azure services. Unlike storing secrets in code or configuration files, Key Vault ensures secure retrieval and centralized management, which is a best practice for cloud security.

113. You need to back up Azure virtual machines and restore them if needed. What should you use?

A. Azure Monitor
B. Recovery Services Vault
C. Azure DNS
D. Azure Policy

Answer: B. Recovery Services Vault
Reasoning: Recovery Services Vault is used to manage backup and recovery operations for Azure resources. It stores recovery points and enables restore operations. Azure Backup uses this vault to protect data from accidental deletion, corruption, or disaster. Monitoring, DNS, and Policy do not provide backup functionality.

114. You want to track and control Azure spending using budgets and alerts. What should you use?

A. Azure Monitor
B. Azure Cost Management
C. Azure DNS
D. Azure Policy

Answer: B. Azure Cost Management
Reasoning: Azure Cost Management allows tracking, analyzing, and optimizing cloud spending. It supports budgets, cost alerts, and detailed cost breakdowns. This helps organizations avoid overspending and allocate costs effectively. Azure Monitor tracks performance, while Policy enforces governance rules.

115. You need to query all Azure resources across subscriptions quickly. What should you use?

A. Azure Resource Graph
B. Azure Monitor
C. Azure Backup
D. Azure DNS

Answer: A. Azure Resource Graph
Reasoning: Azure Resource Graph enables fast querying of resource metadata across multiple subscriptions using KQL. It is optimized for large-scale environments and helps with inventory management, compliance, and auditing. Azure Monitor queries logs, not resource inventory.

116. You want to enforce compliance rules like allowed locations and required tags. What should you use?

A. Azure Monitor
B. Azure Policy
C. NSG
D. Azure DNS

Answer: B. Azure Policy
Reasoning: Azure Policy enforces organizational standards and evaluates compliance. It can deny non-compliant deployments or audit them. Policies are widely used for governance in enterprise environments. NSGs handle network security, not compliance rules.

117. You need to control access to Azure resources based on roles. What should you use?

A. Azure Monitor
B. RBAC
C. Azure DNS
D. Azure Backup

Answer: B. RBAC

Reasoning: Role-Based Access Control allows assigning permissions based on predefined roles like Owner, Contributor, or Reader. It ensures users have only the access they need. RBAC is a core concept in AZ-104 and critical for securing Azure environments.

118. You want to automatically scale virtual machines based on demand. What should you use?

A. Availability Set
B. VM Scale Set
C. Azure Policy
D. Azure DNS

Answer: B. VM Scale Set
Reasoning: Virtual Machine Scale Sets allow automatic scaling based on metrics such as CPU usage or request count. They ensure applications can handle increased load while optimizing cost during low usage. Availability Sets improve availability but do not scale automatically.

119. You need centralized network security filtering for multiple VNets. What should you use?

A. NSG
B. Azure Firewall
C. Azure Monitor
D. Azure DNS

Answer: B. Azure Firewall
Reasoning: Azure Firewall provides centralized network security across multiple VNets. It allows defining and enforcing policies from a single location. NSGs are applied at subnet or NIC level, while Firewall provides centralized control.

120. You need to connect on-premises infrastructure to Azure securely over the internet. What should you use?

A. ExpressRoute
B. VPN Gateway
C. Load Balancer
D. Azure Monitor

Answer: B. VPN Gateway
Reasoning: VPN Gateway establishes encrypted tunnels over the internet between on-premises and Azure. It is cost-effective and commonly used for hybrid cloud connectivity. ExpressRoute is private but requires dedicated circuits.

121–140 (Expert-Level Scenario Questions)
121. You need to restrict VM deployment to only approved sizes and regions. What should you use?

A. Azure Monitor

B. Azure Policy
C. NSG
D. Azure Backup

Answer: B. Azure Policy
Reasoning: Azure Policy can define rules that restrict VM sizes and deployment regions. It ensures compliance with organizational standards and cost control.

122. You want to provide temporary access to a storage account. What should you use?

A. Access keys
B. SAS token
C. Azure Policy
D. NSG

Answer: B. SAS token
Reasoning: SAS tokens provide limited, time-bound access without exposing storage account keys.

123. You need to ensure high availability across regions. What should you use?

A. Availability Set
B. Traffic Manager
C. NSG
D. Azure Monitor

Answer: B. Traffic Manager
Reasoning: Traffic Manager distributes traffic across regions, ensuring failover and global availability.

124. You want to monitor inbound and outbound network traffic. What should you use?

A. NSG Flow Logs
B. Azure Policy
C. Azure Backup
D. DNS

Answer: A. NSG Flow Logs
Reasoning: NSG Flow Logs capture network traffic metadata, helping analyze and troubleshoot traffic patterns.

125. You need to secure web apps against attacks. What should you use?

A. NSG
B. WAF
C. NAT Gateway

D. Azure Monitor

Answer: B. WAF
Reasoning: Web Application Firewall protects against common web vulnerabilities like SQL injection and XSS.

126. You need to store unstructured data like videos and images. What should you use?

A. Blob Storage
B. Table Storage
C. Queue Storage
D. File Storage

Answer: A. Blob Storage
Reasoning: Blob Storage is optimized for large unstructured data and is widely used for media storage.

127. You want to route traffic through a firewall appliance. What should you use?

A. NSG
B. Route Table (UDR)
C. Azure Monitor
D. DNS

Answer: B. Route Table (UDR)
Reasoning: UDR allows directing traffic through network virtual appliances such as firewalls.

128. You need to manage secrets securely. What should you use?

A. Azure Key Vault
B. Azure Monitor
C. Azure DNS
D. Azure Backup

Answer: A. Azure Key Vault
Reasoning: Key Vault securely stores secrets, keys, and certificates.

129. You need to analyze logs using queries. What language is used?

A. SQL
B. KQL
C. Python
D. Java

Answer: B. KQL
Reasoning: KQL is used in Azure Monitor and Log Analytics for querying logs.

130. You want to protect against accidental deletion of resources. What should you use?

A. Tag
B. Resource Lock
C. NSG
D. Azure Monitor

Answer: B. Resource Lock
Reasoning: Resource locks prevent deletion or modification.